THE FOOTBALL BOOK

A complete A-to-Z informal encyclopedia of football, covering the famous stars, teams, coaches, rules and strategies, and great moments on the field. Lavishly illustrated with photographs, drawings, and diagrams.

THE FOOTBALL BOOK

by Larry Lorimer and John Devaney

Random House New York

illustrated with drawings by Charles McVicker, diagrams, and photographs

Revised edition 1979
Copyright © 1977, 1979 by Random House, Inc.

All rights reserved under International and Pan-American
Copyright Conventions. Published in the United States by
Random House, Inc., New York, and simultaneously in Canada
by Random House of Canada Limited, Toronto.

Library of Congress Cataloging in Publication Data

Lorimer, Lawrence T   The football book.

Includes index.
Summary: An encyclopedia of football including the stars, the great moments, early history, records, rivalries, and
important plays.
1. Football—Dictionaries, Juvenile. [1. Football—Dictionaries] I. Devaney, John, joint author. II. Title.
GV950.7.L6   796.33′2′03   77-74461
ISBN 0-394-83574-3 ISBN 0-394-93574-8 lib. bdg.

Manufactured in the United States of America   1 2 3 4 5 6 7 8 9 0

Photo credits can be found on page 157.

LET'S HUDDLE

Before every football play there is a huddle. The quarterback tells his teammates where they should go on the play and what they should do.

This is the authors' huddle—our way to tell you where you should go from here to use this book. As you may already have seen, there are nearly 200 entries arranged alphabetically, from *Alabama* to *zone defense*. If you're checking on a particular football star or team, however, you should consult the index, because many names appear in more than one entry.

We have designed this book to be an introduction to many kinds of football information. For those who are learning to play the game there are illustrated entries on blocking, tackling, passing, kicking, and the techniques of playing each position. For those who want to know more about the exciting history of the game, there are entries on the great events, the teams, and the stars. And for those who are watching the game in person or on television, there are entries on the terms that football players use and the strategies that coaches and quarterbacks follow.

Finally, this is also a book for fans who don't want to know anything in particular but who will find it a pleasure to browse through the pages between games or between seasons. We think the game should be fun as well as educational, and we hope this book provides every reader with both information and fun.

—LARRY LORIMER
JOHN DEVANEY

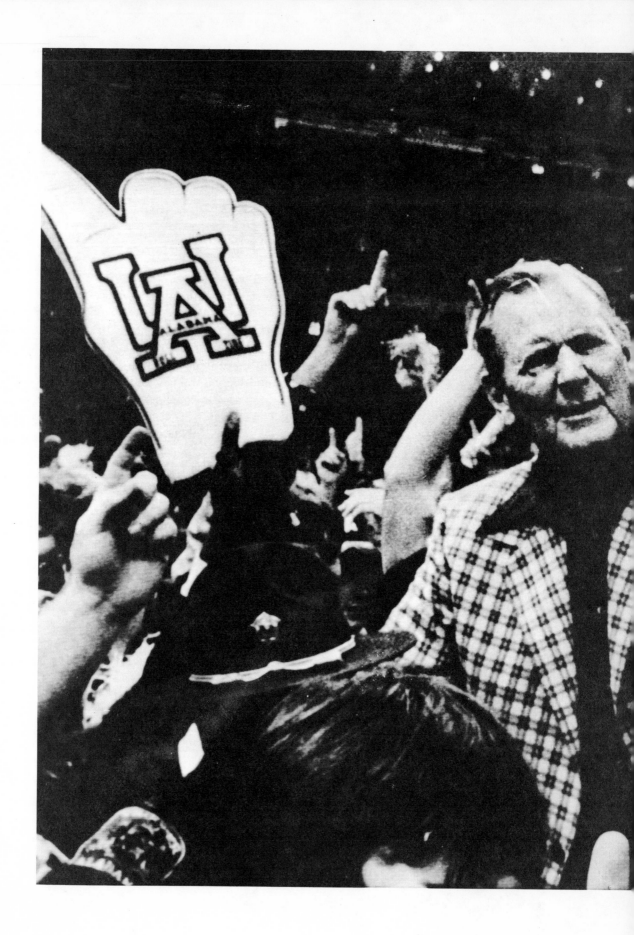

Alabama, University of

On New Year's Day, 1979, the University of Alabama football team lined up against Penn State for the Sugar Bowl game in New Orleans. The stands were filled with 'Bama fans who hoped that *this* year their team would rank number one in the college football polls.

Penn State was ranked number one in the polls before the game. But Alabama was number two. If 'Bama could win, it might become the national champion. One man who especially wanted a victory was Alabama coach Bear Bryant. He had coached the Crimson Tide for twenty-one years, and his 1961 team had been ranked number one. But he would soon retire, and he wanted one more national championship team.

From the beginning, the game was a defensive battle. At the end of three quarters, Alabama led, 14–7. But then Penn State began to move. Twice in the fourth quarter they carried the ball to the one-yard line. But twice the Alabama defenders kept them from making the goal.

At game's end, it was still 14–7, and the Alabama players carried Bear Bryant off the field on their shoulders. The next week, the Associated Press poll named Alabama the national champion.

Coach Bear Bryant is carried off the field in triumph after Alabama beat Penn State in the 1979 Sugar Bowl.

9

In more than twenty years at Alabama, Coach Bryant had become the most successful coach in college football. The Crimson Tide was usually the strongest team in the South, and nearly every year it played in a major bowl game. Bryant helped develop three of the greatest passing quarterbacks in college football history: Joe Namath, Steve Sloan, and Ken Stabler. Both Namath and Stabler went on to become pro stars and play for Super Bowl winners.

The University of Alabama is in Tuscaloosa. Home football games are played in Denny Stadium, which seats 59,000 fans. The school colors are crimson and white.

All-America Football Conference

A professional league organized in 1946 with eight teams—Brooklyn, Buffalo, Chicago, Cleveland, Los Angeles, Miami, New York, and San Francisco. The AAFC lasted from 1946 to 1949. It was dominated by the Cleveland Browns, who won 52 of their 58 games and wound up with the league championship every season. The Browns were one of the few AAFC teams that drew enough fans to make money. Before the 1950 season the league broke up. Three of its teams —the Baltimore Colts (formerly the Miami Seahawks), the Browns, and the San Francisco 49ers—joined the National Football League.

All-America team

A team of college all-stars chosen at the end of the season by a group of experts—usually sportswriters or coaches. Most modern All-America teams have 22 or 24 players, one at each offensive and defensive position and perhaps a punter and a place-kicker. The first well-known All-America team was chosen by Walter Camp in 1889. (*See* Camp, Walter.)

All-Pro team

A team of professional all-stars chosen at the end of the season by a group of experts— usually sportswriters, coaches, or players. Since 1951, All-Pro teams from each conference of the National Football League have played against one another in the Pro Bowl after the regular season and the championship playoffs.

American Football Conference (AFC)

One of the National Football League's two conferences; the other is the National Football Conference (NFC). The two conferences were established in 1970 when the National Football League and the American Football League merged. The 10 AFL teams

were joined by 3 NFL teams to make up the AFC. In 1976 the Tampa Bay Buccaneers came into the AFC as its 14th team. In 1977 Tampa Bay shifted to the NFC and the Seattle Seahawks replaced it in the AFC.

The AFC is divided into three divisions—Eastern, Central, and Western. Each year the top team of the AFC meets the top team of the NFC in the Super Bowl for the championship of the NFL. (*See* National Football League; Super Bowl.)

American Football League (AFL)

In 1960, when the AFL began, the league boldly announced that it would soon be as good as the 40-year-old National Football League.

The AFL started with eight teams. In the Eastern Division were the Boston (later New England) Patriots, the Buffalo Bills, the Houston Oilers, and the New York Titans (later Jets). In the Western Division were the Dallas Texans (later the Kansas City Chiefs), the Denver Broncos, the Los Angeles (later San Diego) Chargers, and the Oakland Raiders. Afterward, the league added the Miami Dolphins and the Cincinnati Bengals.

At first, the play in the AFL was ragged. But many fans loved AFL games. With such passers as Kansas City's Len Dawson and Houston's George Blanda, the teams played a razzle-dazzle, wide-open offense. Often they scored 30 or 40 points a game. "You never know what's going to happen next," said AFL fans. By comparison, the low-scoring NFL games seemed as mild as warm milk.

The players were glad there were two leagues. By negotiating with a team in each league, they could force the teams to pay higher and higher salaries. The leagues

The AFL meets the NFL at the Super Bowl.

fought for good new players. Sometimes they even "kidnapped" a college star so that he couldn't sign with the other league.

"This battling will bankrupt both of us," said some of the wiser owners. In 1966 the leagues finally made peace. They agreed not to fight each other to get players. And at the end of each season the AFL's best team would play the NFL's best team for the world's championship. That game soon became known as the Super Bowl.

The NFL, to the delight of its fans, won the first two Super Bowls, in 1967 and 1968. Then the AFL's Jets, led by Joe Namath, shocked the NFL by beating the NFL's Colts, 16–7, in Super Bowl III. In Super Bowl IV, the AFL champion won again; the Chiefs beat the Vikings in a resounding 23–7 victory.

At last the AFL stood even with the older NFL. But that 1969 season was the last one for the AFL. In 1970 the two leagues merged. The new National Football League had two conferences. The American Football Conference (AFC) was made up of the ten AFL teams, plus three from the NFL.

Atlanta Falcons

The Minnesota Vikings' quarterback, Fran Tarkenton, ducked into the huddle. He had to decide what play to call. Should he try a pass? Or should he try a run?

The Vikings trailed by six points in this 1973 game against the Atlanta Falcons. The Vikings were one of the best teams in the NFL, on their way to the Super Bowl. The Falcons were only a so-so team, with a 6–3 record. But now, while more than 55,000 Atlanta fans watched, the Falcons were beating the proud Vikings. If the Falcons managed to win, it would be the biggest upset in their history.

In the huddle Tarkenton decided to call a pass. As he dropped back, the huge Falcon linemen slammed into the Viking blockers. Suddenly a white-shirted Falcon, wearing number 87, broke through and smashed into

Tarkenton, knocking him to the ground.

Number 87 was the huge 6-foot-5, 265-pound Claude Humphrey, the Falcons' defensive end. He was a star performer in that 1973 game, a game which the Falcons finally won, 20–14. They finished the season with a 9–5 record, their best ever. It was a record that gave them second place in the National Football Conference's Western Division.

That was an unusually good record for the Falcons. They had joined the NFL in 1966, and nearly every season had been a losing one. On defense the Falcons were imposing. Their pass rushers—Humphrey, defensive end John Zook, and linebacker Tommy Nobis—were among the best in the league. But the Falcon offense usually failed to put enough points on the scoreboard.

The Falcons play in Atlanta–Fulton County Stadium, which seats 60,489. The Falcon colors are the colors of the falcon, a fierce bird of prey: red, black, white, and old gold.

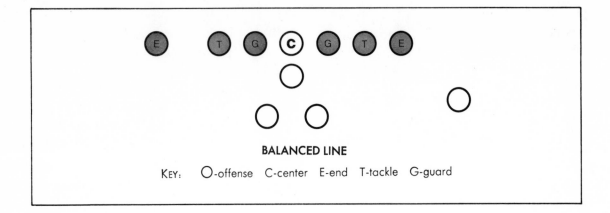

BALANCED LINE

KEY: O-offense   C-center   E-end   T-tackle   G-guard

audible

A play called by the quarterback at the line of scrimmage. The quarterback calls an audible if he sees that the defense is set to stop the play he called in the huddle. For example, suppose a pass play has been called in the huddle but the defense is set up to prevent any pass. Then the quarterback can bark out signals for the new play—perhaps a running play up the middle, where the defense is weakest. Audibles give a quarterback a chance to second-guess the defense.

balanced attack

An offense that is effective on both passing and running plays. A team with a balanced attack has a great advantage over the defense. It is likely to be more successful than a team that is strong in one part of the game and weak in the other.

balanced line

An offensive alignment in which there are three linemen on each side of the center. Most modern formations call for a balanced line. (*See* diagram above.)

Baltimore Colts

Johnny Unitas stared at the other Colt players ringed around him. "Now," he said in his rasping voice, "we're going to find out what we're made of."

The Colts stood under the glare of the Yankee Stadium lights on a dark afternoon in December 1958. The New York Giants were leading the Colts, 17–14, with only a minute and 56 seconds left in this game for the championship of the NFL. The ball sat on the Colt 14-yard line, 86 yards from where the Colts wanted to be. In the next few minutes millions of fans watching on TV would also find out what Unitas and the Colts were made of.

With time clicking away, Unitas knew he had to pass. The Colt quarterback threw short passes to his two favorite receivers, Ray Berry and Lenny Moore. The Colts moved 73 yards to the Giants' 13. Then, with the clock blinking off the final seconds,

Steve Myhra kicked a field goal. The game was tied, 17–17. For the first time ever, an NFL game went into sudden-death overtime. The first team to score would be the NFL champion.

The Giants took the kickoff. The Colt defense reared up to stop the Giants just inches shy of a first down. The Giants punted to the Colt 20. On the 20, Unitas took charge again. He mixed runs by his plunging fullback, Alan "the Horse" Ameche, and passes to Moore and Berry. The Colts moved to the Giant 1-yard line. From there Ameche burst into the end zone for a 23–17 victory. The game became known as "the greatest football game ever played," and the Colts were the winners, claiming their first NFL championship.

The first Colt team was organized in 1947, when the bankrupt Miami Seahawk franchise of the one-year-old All-America Football Conference was moved to Baltimore. In 1950 the league folded. The Colts —along with the Cleveland Browns and the San Francisco 49ers—moved to the NFL. But in their first season the Colts lost 11 of 12 games and dropped out of the league.

For two years Baltimore fans pined for an NFL team. In 1953, as proof of their devotion, they even bought 15,000 season tickets for a team that didn't exist. Impressed, the NFL shifted the Dallas Texans to Baltimore for the '53 season. They became the new Colts.

By 1957 coach Weeb Ewbank had built the Colts into one of the best teams in the NFL. After the overtime thriller of 1958, the Colts repeated as NFL champs in 1959, beating the Giants once more. This time they won, 31–16. In 1964, with Unitas still throwing passes, the Colts secured the NFL's Western Conference title but lost the championship game to Cleveland, 27–0. In 1968 the Colts avenged that loss by beating Cleveland, 34–0, for the NFL title. Then they played the New York Jets, champions of the American Football League in the

Colt fullback Alan Ameche goes through the hole opened up by his teammates, scoring the famous "sudden death" touchdown.

Super Bowl. There they were upset by Joe Namath and his underdog Jets, 16–7.

In 1970 the Colts won their conference championship in the enlarged NFL and got another chance. They took on the Dallas Cowboys in Super Bowl V. The Cowboys jumped to a 6–0 lead. Then came one of the freakiest plays in Super Bowl history. Unitas aimed a pass at receiver Eddie Hinton. The ball tipped off Hinton's fingers, was tipped again by a Dallas defender, then plopped into the hands of Colt tight end John Mackey. Mackey raced 50 yards for a touchdown to tie the game, 6–6.

With only nine seconds left, the game was again tied, 13–13. The Colts had the ball 25 yards from the Cowboys' goal line. Baltimore sent in rookie kicker Jim O'Brien to try for a field goal that would win the game. O'Brien had missed an extra-point kick earlier in the game, and the Cowboys shouted out insulting reminders of his previous flub. But this time O'Brien kicked the ball between the uprights for a 16–13 Colt victory.

During Unitas's declining years, the Colts slid downhill. But by 1975 they had a new passer, the fiery Bert Jones, plus another rampaging runner, Lydell Mitchell. So in 1975, and again in 1976, the Colts won the AFC's Eastern Division championship. But both years they were bumped out of the playoffs by the Pittsburgh Steelers.

The Colts play in Memorial Stadium, which holds 60,020. The team's colors are royal blue, white, and silver.

Baugh, Sammy

The Washington Redskin coach drew the play on the blackboard with a piece of chalk. Lanky end Wayne Millner and a rookie passer named Sammy Baugh were watching him.

15

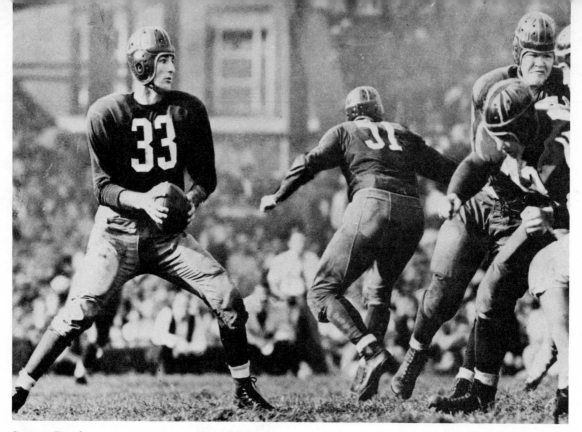

Sammy Baugh prepares to toss one of his famous passes in a 1942 game between the Redskins and the Chicago Bears.

"Wayne," said the coach, "you will take ten steps downfield, then hook back to here." The coach drew an X on the board.

"Sammy," the coach continued, "when Wayne reaches that X, I want you to hit him with the ball right in the eye."

"Sure, Coach," drawled Baugh. "Which eye?"

All during his career Sammy Baugh snapped passes with that kind of bull's-eye accuracy. In his first NFL game he completed 11 of 16 passes. In his first pro season he passed the Redskins to the championship of the NFL East.

They met the top Western Division team, the Chicago Bears, in the game for the 1937 NFL championship. With the score 0–0, the Redskins were penned back on their 9-yard line. Baugh stepped into the end zone as though to punt. He took the snap from center, faked a kick, then arched a long pass to Cliff Battles for a 42-yard gain. The Redskins marched through the stunned Bears for a touchdown and were on their way to a 28–21 victory and the NFL championship.

Sammy Baugh grew up in Texas. Determined to make the Sweetwater High School team, he threw footballs at an auto tire swinging from the limb of a tree. A sportswriter saw him throwing and nicknamed him "Slingin' Sam."

Slingin' Sam ran, kicked, passed, and intercepted passes as the quarterback and safetyman for Texas Christian University. Redskin owner George Preston Marshall signed Sammy for what was considered big money in 1937—$8,000 a year. Sam proved to be worth every nickel. In Baugh's first ten seasons the Redskins won the East title five times and the world's championship twice. (*See* Washington Redskins.)

Baugh set records that still stand—such as the most seasons leading the league in passing (six times). In 1945 he completed seven of every ten passes, a record that few have even approached. But because today's passers throw more often than he did, he is ranked only 20th on the Hall of Fame list of passers.

Baugh, unlike today's pro quarterbacks,

played the full 60 minutes of the game. On defense he was a safetyman. He intercepted four passes in one NFL game. He was also the Redskin punter. His punting average, 45 yards a boot, is another pro record that still stands.

Sammy Baugh retired from the Redskins after the 1952 season. He became a cowboy on a ranch he owned in Texas. Later he coached several pro teams. But none of his players could do all of the things that Sammy Baugh could do—nor could they do most of them as well.

Big Eight

See conferences.

Big Ten

See conferences.

Biletnikoff, Fred

In the huddle Ken Stabler, the Oakland quarterback, glanced at his wide receiver, Fred Biletnikoff. "Do you want anything?" Stabler asked.

Fred nodded. He knew what Stabler meant. Was there a special pass pattern he wanted to run?

"Post," Fred said in his soft-spoken way. Somehow the stocky, worried-looking man didn't have the appearance of a skillful and elusive pass receiver.

The Raiders broke out of the huddle. From above them came the roar of 100,000 fans gathered in Pasadena's Rose Bowl for the 1977 Super Bowl. The Oakland Raiders were leading the Minnesota Vikings, 10–0. The ball was 18 yards from the Viking goal line. Stabler was going to pass. And Fred Biletnikoff had called for the pass pattern he wanted to run—a "post" pattern, a slant toward the goal posts.

Stabler ran back to pass, while Fred gal-loped toward the goal posts. Stabler threw so low that the ball seemed to clip the grass. Somehow Fred snared the ball at his shoe tops with a 200-pound Viking riding on his back. Fred crashed to the ground on the 1-foot line, but he held on to the ball.

From there the Raiders smashed through for another touchdown to lead, 16–0. And they went on to crush the Vikings, 32–14. Fred caught four passes, a low total for him, but three of those four catches had placed the Raiders close enough to score. He was voted the game's most valuable player.

He had fooled the Vikings, as he had fooled so many defenders, with his seemingly plodding way of running a pattern. The Vikings had put two men on the speedy Cliff Branch, but only one on Fred. "He runs the hundred-yard dash in a week," a wit once

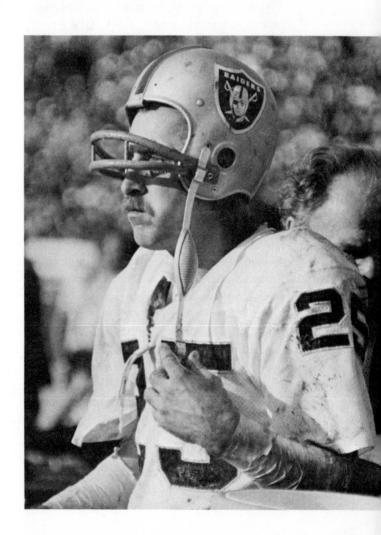

said of Fred, "but he could shake off his shadow if he had to."

Fred had been shaking off defenders since he was a boy chasing passes on the sandlots of Erie, Pennsylvania. At Florida State he was an All-America end. In 1965 he joined the Raiders. Season after season he was among the league's top pass catchers. In 1971 he led the NFL with 61 catches. "Fred," said Raider coach John Madden, "can catch anything he can touch. That's no accident. He doesn't think of anything but catching the ball."

"Pass catching is reflexes, the hands and eyes working together," Fred once said. "I punch a light punching bag. The bag comes back at different angles and that helps the coordination between my hands and my eyes."

With Fred as their most reliable pass catcher, the Raiders won the AFC Western title five straight years from 1972 to 1976. (*See* Oakland Raiders.) By 1976 Fred ranked sixth on the all-time list of pass catchers. He had caught more passes than any other active pass catcher except Charley Taylor, the all-time number one receiver.

Blanda, George

The Oakland Raiders seemed to be sure losers, trailing 20–13 late in the game. And their number one passer, Daryle Lamonica, had just limped to the bench with an injury. He was through for the afternoon.

Into this 1970 game against Cleveland trotted the 43-year-old George Blanda, Oakland's number two passer. With the exception of Lou "the Toe" Groza, George was the oldest player in the history of the NFL. But Groza had come into games only to kick field goals. Blanda stood in the pocket and threw passes, facing the grim charges of burly linemen young enough to be his sons.

George had entered another game a week earlier and kicked a field goal with only three seconds left. His kick had given the

Raiders a "miracle" 17–17 tie. Surely even he couldn't pull a miracle two weeks in a row.

But he could!

Minutes after entering the Cleveland game, George directed the Raiders to within 14 yards of a touchdown. Then he whisked a pass to Warren Wells for a touchdown. George kicked the extra point and the score was tied, 20–20. But George wasn't through. The Raiders got the ball again. And with three seconds to go he kicked a 52-yard field goal to win the game.

In that 1970 season George won or tied six straight games by tossing for touchdowns or kicking field goals and extra points. The Associated Press named him "Athlete of the Year."

George Blanda played in more pro games than any other player—340 games from 1949 through 1975. Born in Youngwood,

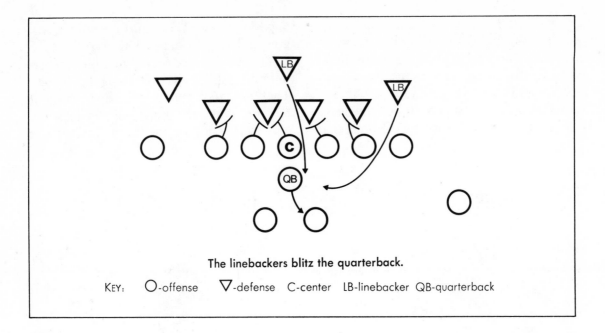

The linebackers blitz the quarterback.

KEY: ○-offense   ▽-defense   C-center   LB-linebacker   QB-quarterback

Pennsylvania, he was an All-America passer for the University of Kentucky. From 1949 to 1958 he tossed passes for the Chicago Bears. He "retired" for the 1959 season, then "unretired" to join the new American Football League as the number one passer for the Houston Oilers. He also kicked field goals for the Houston team. In 1961 he kicked a 55-yard field goal, an AFL record. By 1966, though, his arm seemed worn out. The Oilers traded him to the Raiders, where he became their field-goal kicker and number two quarterback.

Year after year, as George got older, people said he was through. But each season he kicked field goals and threw passes that won games for the Raiders. In fact, the Raiders were in the playoffs every season from 1967 to 1975.

At the start of the 1976 season, the Raiders finally let Blanda go. They said he was "too old," even though he had scored at least one point in every one of his last 69 games. He was the leading scorer of all time. In 26 NFL-AFL seasons he had scored nine touchdowns, kicked 943 extra points and 335 field goals for a total of 2,002 points. The record will stand until some other age-less player is able to play 20 or more seasons, scoring in every game. But that is not likely to happen very soon.

blitz

A defensive trick in which a linebacker or a defensive back charges into the offense's backfield to tackle the ball carrier or passer. Since the linebackers and defensive backs don't usually charge, the blitz is often an unwelcome surprise to the offensive team.

blocking

For the offensive team, blocking is the most important skill in football. A good team may have a great passer, a strong running back, and good pass receivers. But none of these men will ever score unless the rest of the team knows how to block. Without blockers the ball carriers would be tackled before they got by the line of scrimmage.

The main purpose of blocking is to keep the tacklers of the defensive team away from the man with the ball. All ten offensive players who do not have the ball should be watching for chances to block. But the most important blockers are the offensive linemen: the two tackles, two guards, the center, and usually one end. On every play these men line up against the defensive linemen, who are the biggest, meanest tacklers on the opposing team. They must keep these aggressive tacklers from the ball carrier.

The rules of football say that the blockers must do their jobs without using their hands. They must not grab a defensive player or hold him with their arms, and they must not lock their hands together to use as a club. If

Three-point stance

Blocker (right) drives into a tackler.

Cross-body block

20

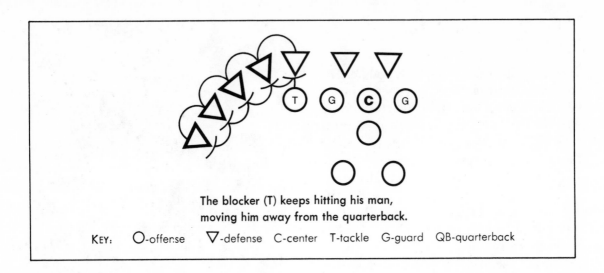

The blocker (T) keeps hitting his man,
moving him away from the quarterback.

KEY: O-offense ▽-defense C-center T-tackle G-guard QB-quarterback

they are caught doing any of these things, the play will be stopped and their team will receive a penalty. (Defensive players—the tacklers—can use their hands.)

To make a good block, the offensive lineman must first learn to take a correct stance. Almost all coaches recommend the three-point stance. The player plants his feet about as far apart as his shoulders, with one foot slightly behind the other. Then he bends at the knees and leans forward from the waist, placing one hand on the ground with fingers spread. He puts just enough weight on the hand so that the defensive player will not be able to push him over backward. His other arm should rest easily against the inside of his leg. The blocker must be careful to line up so that no part of his body is ahead of the ball or he will be called for an offside violation and his team will be penalized.

At the snap of the ball, the lineman drives forward with short digging steps. His hands come up to his chest with his elbows spread wide and he crashes into the defensive player, aiming for the player's waist. A good blocker tries to stay on his feet and remain in contact with his man, continuing to push him away from the ball or the direction of the play.

A good lineman must always know what play has been called. If his team is passing, his job is to protect the passer. Then he may back up a step or two after hitting the defensive man, helping to form a "pocket" for the passer. If the plan is to send a running back through the line, the blocker may have the job of blocking a defensive player to the left or right to open a "hole" for the ball carrier. On this kind of play the blocker must be very aggressive. He has to get himself into position quickly to drive the defensive player in the desired direction.

In some running plays two or three blockers are assigned to pull out of their positions on the line and run ahead of the ball carrier as an escort. Their job is to open a path for the runner, throwing a block at the first tackler who comes near. If possible, these blockers use the same technique as the blocking linemen, trying to meet the tackler head-on with a low charge. But it's not always possible to get into position for such a block. The blocker may then use a cross-body block, throwing his body across the path of the tackler, trying to roll into him between his knees and his waist. In the open field, blockers must be careful never to block from the back. This is called clipping. It is a violation of the rules and could cause serious injury.

bomb

A long pass designed to score a touchdown on a single play.

Bradshaw, Terry

Terry Bradshaw ducked into the huddle. The scoreboard high above him glittered in the late-afternoon gloom. It was the third down. And the Pittsburgh Steelers needed 25 yards for a first down. Worst of all, they trailed the Houston Oilers by two touchdowns.

Terry tried to think of a play. His teammates stared at the young quarterback—this was only his second season in the NFL. "Call something," one of the older Steelers growled. Terry began to stammer.

"I'll call the play," a veteran said finally. He called a play, but it didn't work. The Steelers lost, 29–3.

After that game in 1971, a Steeler told reporters, "We can't win because our quarterback is dumb."

The label "dumb quarterback" would stick to Terry Bradshaw for years. He had come to the Steelers from Louisiana Tech as college football's best passer, and had been the first player drafted.

"I will make Pittsburgh a winner," he said. But instead, he made himself a reputation—as the quarterback who could throw the ball but couldn't call plays.

Gradually, things got better. The Steelers acquired some talented new players, including running-back Franco Harris and receiver Lynn Swann. And Terry Bradshaw gradually learned how to "read" defenses and spot the open receiver. When the defenders bunched up to stop the charges of Franco Harris, Terry threw passes over their heads. The Steelers began to win.

Pittsburgh made the playoffs in 1972 and again in '73. Then after the 1974 season they played their way to the Super Bowl and beat the Vikings, 16–6, for the championship, the Steelers' first ever.

In 1975 the Steelers were back to win their second Super Bowl in a row. Terry fired one 64-yard touchdown pass to Lynn Swann just as he was knocked unconscious by a Dallas tackler. He spent most of the rest of the game on the bench, but the Steelers won, 21–10.

The Steelers' quarterback Terry Bradshaw drops back to throw a pass against the Dallas Cowboys in the 1979 Super Bowl.

Terry lived on a big ranch in Louisiana, near where he grew up, with his second wife, ice-skater Jo Jo Starbuck. In the off-season, he sang country and western songs for a recording company. "One day," he said, "I hope I'll be as famous as a singer as I am now as a football player."

In 1978 the Steelers made the playoffs for the seventh straight season. Against Dallas once more in the Super Bowl, Terry had a terrific day. He threw two touchdown passes and was the game's Most Valuable Player. The Steelers beat the Cowboys, 35–31, and became the first team ever to win three Super Bowls.

"Some people were still saying I was dumb

until we won the third Super Bowl," Terry said. "Isn't it amazing how I got so smart so fast?"

Brown, Jim

The Cleveland runner struck into the Giants' line. The New York Giants' burly linebacker, Sam Huff, wrestled him to the ground. For the second straight time Jim Brown, Cleveland's record-breaking runner, had been stopped for no gain.

"Brown, you stink!" shouted Sam Huff, who prided himself on stopping Jim Brown.

On the next play Jim Brown, ball nestled under his right arm, dashed toward Huff. Huff reached out to grab Brown. But Brown's knees, driving like pistons, flashed through Huff's grasping hands. Brown sped 65 yards for a touchdown. As he crossed the goal line he turned and saw Sam Huff chasing after him. "Hey, Sam," hollered Jim Brown. "How do I smell from here?"

No one ever stopped the speedy 6-foot-2, 230-pound Jim Brown for very long. Stopping him was like stopping an express train. In nine NFL seasons he gained 12,312 yards, more than any rusher before or since. In comparison, O.J. Simpson gained fewer than 10,000 yards in his first eight seasons. On an average rush O.J. gained 4.8 yards. Jim Brown gained 5.3 yards, a half-yard more. If you count pass catches and kick returns, Jim Brown gained more than nine miles during his playing career.

Jim grew up in Manhasset, New York. As a boy he led a stick-swinging street gang. But sports soon drew him away from gang wars. At Manhasset High, and later at Syracuse University, Jim was the best at sports that ranged from baseball to the old Indian game of lacrosse.

An All-America back at Syracuse, he was picked for pro football in 1957 by the Cleveland Browns. Immediately he became the Browns' best runner. In one game he lugged the ball 31 times, a record that stood

for some 15 years. "He's going to wind up punch-drunk if he keeps carrying the ball that often," one coach warned.

But Jim went right on carrying the ball. He led the league in rushing during eight of his nine seasons. Often he tricked opponents by limping back to the huddle after he was hit. His opponents would think he was hurt. But on the next play he would shoot by tacklers with his usual explosive speed and power.

The Browns stood high in the NFL during Jim's career. But they were never the champs until 1964, when they beat the Baltimore Colts, 27–0, for the NFL championship. On that day Jim rampaged for 114 yards on a frozen field. "That was the high point for me," he said later. "We finally won the big one."

In 1965, after leading in the league in rushing (1,544 yards), Jim Brown quit football and became a popular movie actor.

Buffalo Bills

Rawboned Jack Kemp looked at his Buffalo teammates while they waited tensely in their dressing room. From outside they could hear the rising roar of 30,000 fans gathered in the San Diego stadium. The fans were impatient for the kickoff of this battle between the Bills and the San Diego Chargers for the 1965 championship of the American Football League.

"Look," Kemp told the Bills, "let's get a quick lead. With our defense we can win with a three-point field goal."

Minutes later the game began. The massive Buffalo defense flung back the San Diego ball carriers. But Jack Kemp could not move the Bills near the goal line. At the end of the first quarter the score was 0–0.

Then Kemp noticed that the Charger defenders were spreading wide to halt end runs. Kemp began to flip short passes over the middle. The Bills marched to the 18-yard line. From there, Kemp tossed another pass that flanker Ernie Warlick caught for a touchdown. Pete Gogolak, the first of the soccer-style kickers, booted the extra point. The Bills led, 7–0. Later on, Gogolak kicked three field goals. The Bills won by a wide margin, 23–0.

That shutout victory gave the Bills their second straight AFL championship. In 1966 they tried for their third successive win, but were defeated, 31–7, by Kansas City.

During the ten-year history of the AFL the Bills were nearly always high in the standings. They did nearly everything well. There were passers Jack Kemp and Daryle Lamonica, bulldozing runner Cookie Gilchrist, kicker Pete Gogolak, who seldom missed a field goal from inside the 35, and gutty defenders such as giant lineman Tom Sestak and quick pass interceptor Butch Byrd.

In 1970 the Bills trooped into the NFL with the other AFL teams. Their star was O.J. Simpson. In 1973, "the Juice," as other players called him, gained more yards than any rusher ever—2,003. Buffalo finished second in the AFC East. O.J. went on gobbling up yardage season after season but his Bills never reached the Super Bowl. Unfortunately the Bills gave up more points than even the Juice could score.

The Buffalo Bills play in 80,020-seat Rich Stadium, a few miles outside Buffalo, in Orchard Park, New York. The team's colors are scarlet red, royal blue, and white.

bump and run

A technique used by defensive backs to throw off the timing of a pass receiver. The back bumps the receiver near the line of

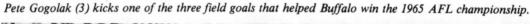

Pete Gogolak (3) kicks one of the three field goals that helped Buffalo win the 1965 AFL championship.

scrimmage before a pass is thrown, then follows him out on his pass pattern. The rules say that the defensive man can bump an eligible receiver only once on a play.

Camp, Walter

Young Walter Camp grew up in New Haven, Connecticut, the home of Yale University. When he was 16, he went to the campus to see a new game played between Yale and Harvard. It was called football, and its rules had been brought over from England. In some ways it was like modern football. It was played on a field of about the same size, and the teams tried to kick the ball over a goal post or run it across the goal line.

But in many ways the game was very different. A touchdown didn't give a team any points. It just gave the team a chance to score by kicking the ball over the goal posts. After every play, the ball was put down between the two teams and they fought over it. This was called the "scrum." Often ten minutes would pass before one team could get the ball out of the pile of players and move it down the field. Harvard won the 1875 game, four goals to none.

The next year, 1876, Yale and Harvard played again. This time Walter Camp was one of the players for Yale. In a tense, exciting game, Yale scored once to win, 1–0. Camp, only 17, was a star. Later that year

he went to a meeting to help establish rules for the new football game. In fact, Walter Camp attended every rules meeting for nearly 50 years. And his ideas helped to make American football a new and exciting game with rules of its own. Camp was the father of American football—as a player, unofficial coach, and rules maker.

In 1880 Camp proposed that the "scrum" be ended. Instead of the teams fighting for the ball, he felt that one team should have possession of it when the play started. He called his new way of starting plays "the scrimmage," and the rules committee adopted it.

But this change brought a new problem. A team could gain possession of the football and hold it for half the game without moving it or scoring. There were many dull, scoreless ties. Both the players and the spectators complained. So Camp suggested that each team be given three plays or "downs" to gain five yards. If the team failed, the other team would get the ball. This new system of downs was tried, and it worked. (Later, a team would get four downs to gain ten yards.)

Little by little, thanks to Walter Camp's imagination, the game developed into American football as we know it today. He had the Yale field marked off into five-yard intervals. He experimented with formations and suggested an early version of the T formation —seven men on the scrimmage line and four in the backfield. He encouraged the adoption of the forward pass. (It was finally accepted in 1907.) And he developed the modern system of scoring—six points for a touchdown, three for a field goal, and so on.

Beginning in 1889, Camp also picked an "All-America" team each year, choosing the best college players at each position. In the early years, most of the All-Americas were from three or four eastern colleges. But by 1924, the year before Camp died, his choices came from all over the country—from the Midwest and the South and even from the Pacific Coast. Football had become a national game for America, and Walter Camp was the man most responsible.

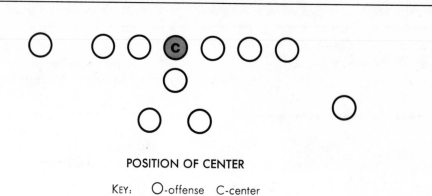

POSITION OF CENTER

KEY: O-offense C-center

center

The center is an offensive lineman who has important blocking responsibilities on nearly every play. (*See* offensive lineman; blocking.) But he has one job that is all his. His position in the line is right over the football, which he puts into play by snapping it back to the quarterback, the punter, or the holder for a place-kick. The center is the only man on offense who is certain to touch the ball on every play. And he must be sure to do his job well. Otherwise his team will suffer from fumbles and blocked kicks.

Most teams use some form of the T formation in which the quarterback lines up just behind the center with his hands extended between the center's legs to receive the ball. A center in the T formation can actually feel the quarterback's hand against the inside of his thigh and can deliver the ball without looking back.

The center takes a different stance from other linemen. His feet are planted farther apart and both hands rest on the ball. If he is right-handed, his right hand rests on the right side of the ball toward the front with his thumb on the front end of the lacing. His

A T-formation quarterback lines up behind the center.

left hand is on the left side of the ball toward the rear with the thumb on the back end of the lacing. For left-handers, the position of the hands is reversed.

On the proper signal—called the "snap count"—the center brings the ball up and back with a slight twist so that the laces of the ball land against the fingertips of the quarterback's right hand. All the time the center is looking upfield, preparing for his blocking assignment. As soon as the ball is snapped, he charges into the defense and carries out his job.

The center must use a different technique in punting or place-kicking situations, when he must snap the ball back 6 to 12 yards. He places his right foot slightly behind the left so that his right arm can swing back as far as possible. He rotates the ball so that the fingers of his right hand are on the laces, and he puts his left hand nearer the front of the ball. His head is down and his eyes are fixed on the target (the punter or holder). At the signal he passes the ball between his legs, using his right hand to supply most of the power. The ball should spiral back to the receiver on a straight line. Perfecting the pass back takes lots of practice, but it's the most important play a center makes. A bad pass from the center may mean a fumble or a blocked kick and put the opposition in position to score easily. The center's long pass backwards can be as important as the quarterback's forward passes.

Chicago Bears

The Chicago Bear players stared at the headline tacked on their locker-room wall:

MARSHALL CALLS BEARS "CRYBABIES"

The year was 1940. During the season, the Bears had lost to Washington, 7–3, after arguing bitterly about a decision by one of the officials. As a result, George Preston Marshall, the owner of the Redskins, had told newspapers that the Bears were "crybabies."

"Crybabies!" a Chicago player growled. "We'll show Marshall and the Redskins we're no crybabies."

And the Bears did—in what may have been the most shockingly lopsided pro football game ever played.

The Bears, NFL Western champions, met the Redskins, NFL Eastern champs, in the 1940 league championship game. The Redskins were favored to win. Their Slingin' Sammy Baugh was the most feared passer in football.

Although the Bears were a young team, they had a very clever quarterback—Sid Luckman. "He never calls a wrong play," said Bear coach George Halas. "It's like having a coach out there on the field."

The Bears also had a young running back. He was tall and slim, weighing only 170 pounds, and he ran with the twisting elusiveness of a snake. "You think you have him," an opponent once said, "but what you grab is empty air." The running back's name was George McAfee.

The Bears had another advantage: as a team they were big. In fact, their fans called them the Monsters of the Midway. (The Midway was an area of Chicago.)

But many experts favored the older, more experienced Redskin players. The Bears ran their plays out of the T formation, a new-fangled idea in 1940. The Redskins, with their conventional single-wing formation, seemed likely to wreck the Bears and put their T-formation plays in the wastepaper basket.

In planning his strategy for the game, Bear coach Halas figured that the Redskins would use the same defensive formation that had beaten the Bears, 7–3, earlier in the season. So Halas gave Luckman T-formation plays that would open holes in the Washington defense.

The Bears received the opening kickoff. On the second play of the game, "Bullet" Bill Osmanski shot through one of those

The elusive George McAfee gains yards for the Bears in their 1940 championship game against the Redskins.

holes in the defense and ran 68 yards for a touchdown. That was only the beginning. The fired-up Bears scored touchdown after touchdown. Some 36,000 Redskin fans sat in stunned surprise, blinking at what was happening to their proud champions.

The Bears roared down the field for 11 touchdowns. After each touchdown they shouted at the Redskins, "Who's a crybaby now?" Finally, after the Bears' 11th touchdown, the referee beckoned to George Halas. "The fans," said the referee, "have kept every football kicked into the stands after each conversion. This is the last football we have. Would you mind asking your boys not to kick for the extra point but to run or pass for it?"

The Bears passed for the extra point. The

final score was 73–0, the most smashing victory in the history of NFL championship games.

George Halas and the Bears had been winning championships ever since the National Football League was born. After World War I Halas became the coach of a company-sponsored team, the Staley Athletic Club in Decatur, Illinois (*See* Halas, George.) In 1920 the Staleys joined the American Professional Football Association, which was later renamed the National Football League. In 1921, the first year of league standings, the Staleys finished first with a 10–1–1 record. In 1922 the Staleys moved to Chicago, and changed their name to the Bears.

During the late 1920s and the 1930s the Bears featured the league's two fanciest and hardest runners: Red Grange and Bronko Nagurski. In 1933 the Bears won the first playoff game for the NFL championship. As the champions of the West, they beat the New York Giants, champions of the East, 23–21, on a last-minute forward pass by Bronko Nagurski.

Then came Sid Luckman and company. They won championships in 1940, 1941, 1943, and 1946. There were less distinguished years until 1956, when the Bears again won in the West but lost the championship game to the Giants, 47–7. The Bears avenged that defeat seven years later in 1963 by beating the Giants, 14–10, for their sixth NFL championship.

In the late 1960s and on into the 1970s the Bears thrilled fans with another great "one play" runner—Gale Sayers. Sayers was faster and more slippery than George McAfee. And there were even bigger players than the Monsters of the Midway who had flourished in the thirties, notably linebackers Dick Butkus and Wally Chambers. In 1976 squat running back Walter Payton led the league in rushing. He went on to become one of the NFL's best, setting a record by

UNBEATEN, UNTIED, AND—OOPS!

Each year only a handful of college teams go through the season unbeaten and untied. A very few of the greatest teams have even played through a whole season without letting anyone score on them. The Michigan team of 1901 scored 516 points and allowed none at all to its opponents.

The 1938 Duke team also had a chance at such a season. It won all of its 1938 games by shutouts. Then the Blue Devils, as they are called, went to the Rose Bowl to play the University of Southern California. In the closing minutes Duke was ahead, 3–0. Then a fourth-string unknown named Doyle Nave came off the Southern Cal bench to throw a series of passes that brought USC all the way downfield. When Southern Cal scored, all of Duke's records went up in smoke. The unknown passer had beaten them *and* scored the only points against them in ten games.

The next season Duke's southern neighbor, Tennessee, made the same mistake of playing one game too many. Tennessee was unbeaten, untied and unscored-upon when it went to the Rose Bowl. Tennessee lost, 14–0. The winner? USC, of course.

gaining 275 yards in one game. During the 1970s the Bears finished in the lower depths of the NFC's Central Division.

The Bears play in Soldier Field, which seats 55,753. The team colors are orange, navy blue, and white.

Cincinnati Bengals

The Oakland Raiders were leading the Cincinnati Bengals, 31–14, at the beginning of the fourth period of this 1975 NFL playoff game. Behind by 17 points, the Bengals seemed sure losers.

Bengal quarterback Ken Anderson told his teammates, "We're not licked yet." Minutes later he flung a pass to flanker Charlie Joiner for a 25-yard touchdown. The score was 31–21. Soon after, Anderson danced back and lined a pass to his favorite receiver, Isaac Curtis, for another touchdown. The score was 31–28. Now Cincinnati was only three points behind, and its offense was red-hot.

But the Oakland defense rose to the challenge. Led by Ted "Mad Stork" Hendricks, Oakland's giant linemen swept in on Cincinnati's Anderson when he ran back to pass. He had to throw hurriedly. His passes fell incomplete. Oakland ran off the field with a 31–28 victory.

"We knew Cincinnati would be tough," said Oakland coach John Madden.

As a matter of fact, the Bengals had always been tough. They joined the American Football League as its tenth team in 1968, and won their very first home game, defeating Denver, 24–10.

The Bengals' first coach was Paul Brown, a stern pilot who had steered the Cleveland Browns to four NFL championships. Brown amazed other coaches with his "nose" for talent. "He can look at a thousand college players and smell out the two or three great ones," the coaches said.

Bengal quarterback Ken Anderson about to fling a pass.

In 1968 and 1969 Brown picked future NFL All-Stars for the Bengals: flanker Bob Trumpy, linebacker Bill Bergey, receiver Isaac Curtis, and quarterback Ken Anderson. In 1970, after the merger of the AFL with the NFL, the Bengals were grouped with the Central Division of the American Football Conference. That first season they won the division title. Their rise to the top was one of the quickest in pro football history.

The Bengals were also division champs in 1973. In 1975 they finished second in their division with an 11–3 record. Again they were one of the eight teams that entered the playoffs. The Bengals didn't get to the Super Bowl, however. They were erased from the playoffs by their narrow 31–28 loss to the Raiders. "We'll be in the Super Bowl one day," Ken Anderson promised.

The Bengals play in Riverfront Stadium, a huge bowl that seats 56,200. The Bengals copy the colors of the tiger: orange, black, and white.

Cleveland Browns

On a wind-swept field in Cleveland the Los Angeles Rams were leading the Cleveland Browns in the 1950 NFL championship game. This was the Browns' first NFL season. Organized in 1946, the Browns had played in the All-America Football Conference, which made its debut that same year. In each of the AAFC's four seasons—from 1946 to 1949—the Browns had been league champions. AAFC fans boasted that the Browns could beat the NFL champs. But NFL fans scoffed. What teams had the Browns beaten? Just other teams in the AAFC—a minor league according to NFL supporters.

In 1950 the AAFC disbanded. The Browns—named for their coach, Paul Brown—joined the National Football League. The Cleveland team had curly-haired Otto Graham at quarterback. He threw passes to two quick receivers, Dante

Otto Graham (left) and Dante Lavelli celebrate their victory in the first AAFC championship game (1946).

Lavelli and Mac Speedie. A twisting runner, Dub Jones (whose son, Bert, would later become an NFL quarterback), ran for long gains. And a bull of a fullback, Marion Motley, tore through the arms of tacklers. In the Browns' first season they finished first in the NFL East. Now they were playing the champions of the West, the high-scoring Los Angeles Rams, for the NFL crown. There was less than two minutes left to play. The Rams led, 28–27. "A good try by the Browns," many fans said, "but the Browns still aren't up to the level of a top NFL team."

Graham began to prove them wrong. He darted short passes to his receivers. He faked passes and ran. The Browns stormed to the Rams' 14-yard line. Only 30 seconds remained. The Browns' field-goal kicker, Lou "the Toe" Groza calmly kicked the ball between the uprights. The Browns had won, 30–28! They had proved just how good they

really were. In their first season in the NFL, they were champions.

Graham, the high-scoring Groza, and the other Browns won the NFL's Eastern title for six straight years—from 1950 to 1955. And in three of those six years they beat the top Western team, becoming world champions.

In 1956 Graham retired. Most of the other original Browns were gone. Paul Brown began to build a new team spearheaded by the greatest ground gainer of all time—the high-stepping, thundering Jim Brown. In 1963, Brown gained 1,863 yards —more than any back before him. In 1964 —under new coach Blanton Collier—the Browns won their fourth NFL title, beating Baltimore, 27–0, in the championship game.

When Jim Brown (who was not related to Paul Brown) retired in 1965, he was succeeded by another slashing runner who led the league in ground gaining. His name was

Leroy Kelly. And Cleveland passers threw the ball to a skinny receiver, Paul Warfield, who was as difficult to cover as a feather in the wind. The Cleveland team won Eastern championships in both 1968 and 1969, but each time the Western champions defeated them in their bid for the NFL title and the right to go to the Super Bowl.

In 1970 the Browns became part of the AFC's Central Division. Pittsburgh won that division title every year from 1972 to 1976. But Cleveland fans still had their hopes, as well as their memories of perhaps the greatest quarterback and the greatest runner of all time—Otto Graham and Jim Brown.

The Browns play in Cleveland Stadium, which seats 80,165. The team's colors are seal brown, burnt orange, and white.

Paul Brown (center), coach of the Browns and later coach of the Cincinnati Bengals.

clipping

A block thrown at a player from behind. Clipping is against football rules and calls for a 15-yard penalty. Clipping is also dangerous, because it is likely to cause knee or leg injuries to the player who is clipped.

coaches

When football first began, there were no coaches. The players ran their own teams. They scheduled their games, planned their strategy, and taught each other how to play. Within a few years, however, graduate students who had played on the team often became unofficial coaches. They taught younger players the fine points of the game.

In the 1890s colleges began to assign a professor to coach football teams after class hours. At first these coaches were more like supervisors. They made sure that players did not misbehave, and they watched for injuries.

But the younger coaches, who had played football in their college days, soon began to work out new plays, plan strategy, and teach young players. Before long the coach became the hub of most college teams. Players came and went, graduating in a few years, but the coach stayed on.

Of all the coaches in football, a few stand out because their teams succeeded or because they introduced new ideas to the game. Probably the most famous are Knute Rockne of Notre Dame (*see* Rockne, Knute) and Vince Lombardi of the Green Bay Packers (*see* Lombardi, Vince).

Of all the early coaches, the most inventive was Amos Alonzo Stagg. His first big coaching job was at the University of Chicago, beginning in 1892. He didn't retire completely from football until the late 1950s, when he was nearly 100 years old. He died in 1965 at the age of 103.

Stagg was the first coach to use the huddle. He also invented dozens of new plays and formations. In 1892 he wrote the first book on football strategy. Much of his material would still be useful today. And he made the University of Chicago, then a member of the Big Ten conference, into a major football power.

Fielding "Hurry Up" Yost coached at the University of Michigan, beginning in 1901. His 1902 team outscored its opponents 516–0, and his Wolverines went five seasons without a single loss. Bob Zuppke at Illinois developed Red Grange, the great running back, in the 1920s and turned out many winning teams. George Halas, the owner of the Chicago Bears, was coach of the first successful NFL team, a post he held for more than 40 years. Other great coaches came from the South, many of whom had played for Dana Bible, a great coach at Tennessee.

In 1946, a professional team was actually named after a coach. The Cleveland Browns got their name from Paul Brown, who developed the team into a consistent winner. He later built the Cincinnati Bengals into a winning team. Many considered Brown the most brilliant football thinker of his time. But he didn't always get along with his players, one reason being that he sent in plays instead of allowing the quarterback to call them.

Some modern college coaches have been the most popular men in their section of the country. Paul "Bear" Bryant at Alabama was a particular favorite. And others such as Woody Hayes at Ohio State and Joe Paterno at Penn State were not far behind.

coffin corner

The corner of the field where the sideline and goal line meet. A punter often aims his kick at the coffin corner, hoping that the ball will bounce out of bounds near the opponent's goal.

conferences

Most college football teams play against other schools in their region of the country. The schools are usually members of a college conference (what the pros would call a league). Each year the team with the best won–lost record against other teams in its conference is crowned the conference champion. Some conference champions represent their conference in post-season bowl games.

The major conferences are:

Atlantic Coast: Clemson, Duke, Maryland, North Carolina, North Carolina State, South Carolina, Virginia, and Wake Forest.

Big Eight: Colorado, Iowa State, Kansas, Kansas State, Missouri, Nebraska, Oklahoma, and Oklahoma State.

Big Ten: Illinois, Indiana, Iowa, Michigan, Michigan State, Minnesota, Northwestern, Ohio State, Purdue, and Wisconsin.

Ivy League: Brown, Columbia, Cornell, Dartmouth, Harvard, Pennsylvania, Princeton, and Yale.

Pacific Eight: California (Berkeley), Oregon, Oregon State, Southern California, Stanford, UCLA, Washington, and Washington State.

Southeastern: Alabama, Auburn, Florida, Georgia, Kentucky, Louisiana State, Mississippi, Mississippi State, Tennessee, and Vanderbilt.

Southwest: Arkansas, Baylor, Houston, Rice, Southern Methodist (SMU), Texas, Texas A & M, Texas Christian (TCU), and Texas Tech.

Western Athletic: Arizona, Arizona State, Brigham Young, Colorado State, New Mexico, Texas–El Paso (UTEP), Utah, and Wyoming.

Some of the major football teams belong to no conference and are called *independents*. They include: Air Force, Army, Georgia Tech, Miami (Florida), Navy, Notre Dame, Penn State, Pittsburgh, Rutgers, Syracuse, and Tulane.

conversion

One name for the try-for-point after a touchdown. (*See* try-for-point.)

cornerback

A defensive back who plays between the linebackers and the safeties. The defensive backfield is made up of two cornerbacks and two safeties. (*See* defensive back.)

Cotton Bowl game

The game played each New Year's Day between major college teams in the Cotton Bowl in Dallas, Texas. The Cotton Bowl is the youngest of the four major bowl games, having started in 1937.

The Cotton Bowl is the official post-season game of the Southwestern Conference. Each year the winning team in the conference appears in the Cotton Bowl game, usually playing a strong team from another part of the country. By far the most frequent visitor to the Cotton Bowl has been the University of Texas, which has appeared 15 times. In recent years, the visiting teams have included such independent teams as Penn State and Notre Dame.

counter play

A play in which a backfield man and one or more blockers move in one direction while the ball carrier moves in the opposite (or "counter") direction. The play is designed to draw the defense in one direction while the ball goes in the other direction, "against the flow."

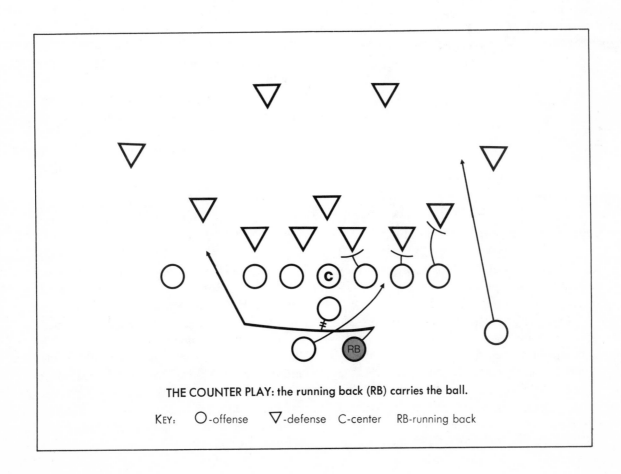

THE COUNTER PLAY: the running back (RB) carries the ball.

KEY: ◯-offense ▽-defense C-center RB-running back

Cox, Fred

Most of the 46,000 chilled people in the Minnesota stadium were standing as the Vikings lined up to try for the field goal. If the Vikings could kick this field goal, they would be almost certain winners of the 1973 playoff game.

The score was Vikings 24, Redskins 20. A three-point field goal would put the Vikings ahead by seven points. Even if Washington scored a last-gasp touchdown, the game would be only tied. Anxious Viking fans gripped their scorecards as they prayed for Fred Cox to make this kick.

The stumpy Fred stood behind the line, eyeing the sharp angle toward the goal posts 30 yards away. He saw the snapback from the center to the holder. Stepping forward, he swung his right foot into the brown pigskin. The ball soared in a high arc, tumbling end over end. Fred watched it float over the goal posts. Up went the arms of the referee. *Three points!* Happy Vikings pounded a smiling Fred on the shoulders. A little later the gun sounded and the Vikings were 27–20 winners.

That field goal represented only three of the hundreds of points that Fred racked up on scoreboards for the Vikings during his long NFL career. Fred grew up in Monongahela, Pennsylvania. In college he kicked field goals for the University of Pittsburgh. He tried out for the Vikings in 1962, but they said he wasn't good enough for the NFL. Fred didn't give up. The next fall he tried out again, and this time he became the Viking kicker. In 1965 he kicked 23 field goals, more than anyone else in the league.

Fred kicked the ball by running straight at it. He wasn't a soccer-style kicker like Kansas City's Jan Stenerud, who came at the ball from the side. Although Fred couldn't kick as far as some of the soccer-style kickers, his kicks were as true as anyone's. In 1969 and 1970 he led the NFL in the number of field goals and in total scoring. During the five-year period from 1969 to 1973, he kicked 170 extra points without a miss. And from 1968 to 1970 he kicked field goals in 31 straight games—an NFL record that was still standing a half-dozen years later. By 1977, having kicked more than 250 field goals and more than 500 extra points for the Vikings, he had scored more points than any active player. And he ranked number three—behind George Blanda and Lou Groza—on the list of the all-time high scorers.

Dallas Cowboys

The Cowboy quarterback, Roger Staubach, stared at the defense of the Miami Dolphins spread out before him. The ball sat just seven yards from a Dallas touchdown in this game—Super Bowl VI.

Roger guessed that the Dolphins would gang up to stop a run. He took the snap from the center and faked giving the ball to running back Calvin Hill. Sure enough, the Dolphins rushed forward to tackle Hill. Roger looked into the end zone. He saw his flanker, Lance Alworth, veer behind a Dolphin defender. Roger looped a pass

The Cowboys' Roger Staubach gets set to throw a pass against the Dolphins in the 1972 Super Bowl.

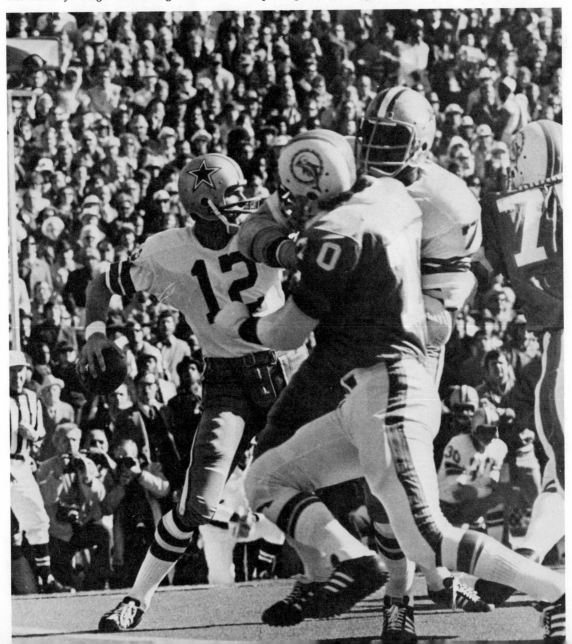

37

A jubilant Coach Landry hugs one of his Cowboys after a big victory.

which Alworth snared for a touchdown. The Cowboys led, 10–0.

They won that Super Bowl game, 24–3, and with it the 1971 NFL championship. Their Doomsday Defense became the first to keep a team from scoring a touchdown in the Super Bowl.

That victory was the peak for a Cowboy team that had gone into 10 playoffs during an 11-year period. The team, owned by millionaire Clint Murchison, Jr., entered the NFL in 1960. It didn't win a single game during its first season. But after that first year, under coach Tom Landry, the Cowboys began to rise. In 1966, with quarterback Dandy Don Meredith, giant tackle Bob Lilly, and other stars, the Cowboys finished first in the NFL East. They faced the Green Bay Packers, the champions of the West, in a game for the championship of the NFL. The winner would go to Super Bowl I.

The Packers beat Meredith and the Cow-

boys, 34–27. That defeat marked the beginning of several years of frustration for the Cowboys and their fans. The next year, 1967, the Cowboys again challenged the Packers for the NFL title and seemed to have the game won, 17–14, in the closing minutes. Then the Packers began a long, crunching drive that ended when Bart Starr plunged for the winning touchdown on the last play of the game.

In 1968 and 1969 the Cowboys lost to the Browns in games for the championship of the NFL's East. In 1970, after the merger of the AFL and NFL, the Cowboys joined the National Football Conference's Eastern Division. That year they won the division championship and went to the Super Bowl. They lost to Baltimore on a last-minute field goal, 16–13. The next season, 1971, they beat Miami to win Super Bowl VI and their first NFL championship.

Then came more years of frustration. In

1972 and 1973 they lost playoff games for the NFC championship. In 1974 they failed to make the playoffs for the only time since 1965. And in 1975 they beat the Rams to win the NFC championship and enter Super Bowl X.

At the Super Bowl they opposed the Pittsburgh Steelers. The Cowboys were behind, 21–17, in the final minute as Staubach steered his team to within 33 yards of the winning touchdown. He floated a long pass toward the end zone, and the huge crowd in Miami's Orange Bowl gripped their programs with wet hands. Then a Steeler leaped to intercept the pass. Again the Cowboys trudged out of a championship game as the losers.

But it was not until after the 1977 season that the Cowboys won their second Super Bowl. They defeated the Denver Broncos by a score of 27–10 in Super Bowl XII. After the 1978 season they had a chance to be the first team to win three Super Bowls as they opposed the AFC champions, the Pittsburgh Steelers, in Super Bowl XIII. The Cowboys came close, but the Steelers won an exciting game, 35–31.

The Cowboys play in Texas Stadium in Irving, a short ride from Dallas. The stadium seats 65,101. The Cowboy colors are royal blue, metallic blue, and white.

dead ball

The ball is dead whenever play stops. This happens when:
1. The referee blows his whistle, ending play.
2. The ball, or the man with the ball, goes out of bounds.
3. The ball hits the goal post.
4. A forward pass falls incomplete.

When the ball is dead, no further motion will count. If a ball carrier fumbles after the whistle, for example, his team keeps possession no matter who picks up the ball.

defensive back

Four of the men on the defensive team are considered part of the backfield. Two are called corner men or cornerbacks, the other two are called safeties. The four defensive backs are mainly responsible for defending against passes thrown by the opposition. When the pass receivers charge downfield,

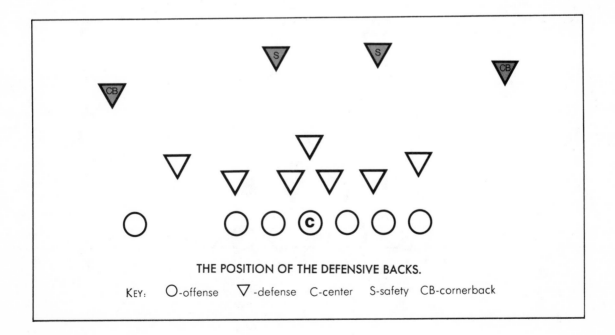

THE POSITION OF THE DEFENSIVE BACKS.

KEY: O-offense ▽-defense C-center S-safety CB-cornerback the defensive backs must keep up with them stride for stride. If the four backs do their job well, the passer may not be able to pass at all. His receivers will be covered. If he does pass, the defenders must make sure that the receiver doesn't catch the ball. A defensive back is always looking for a chance to intercept a pass, but he must learn not to take foolish chances. His first job is to prevent any completions.

Pass receivers are usually the fastest men on the offensive team. So safeties and cornerbacks must be almost as fast. They are not allowed to touch or interfere with the receiver as long as the ball is in the air, so they concentrate on sticking with the receivers and being in a position to knock down the ball. Defensive backs must have good peripheral vision—the ability to see what is going on around them while still keeping their eyes on the receiver.

On some teams the defensive backs cover receivers man to man. They are assigned to one receiver and cover him all the way. Other teams assign the backs to cover zones. Each back is responsible for defending against any pass thrown to a certain area, or zone, of the field. On zone or man-to-man coverage, defensive backs are always worried about long passes. If they fail to bat down a long pass, the other team will often score.

Although defensive backs are usually smaller than others on the defensive team, they must be good tacklers. Sometimes they have to substitute courage for size. If their teammates make a mistake and fail to stop a ball carrier, the defensive backs are the last line of defense. A 180-pound back may have to tackle a 230-pound ball carrier who is running at full speed.

So a good defensive back must have many qualities. He must be fast, have good reactions and eyesight, and he must be a fearless tackler.

defensive lineman

In modern football there are four defensive linemen—two tackles and two ends. Sometimes called the "front four," they are the biggest, meanest tacklers on the team. On almost every play they battle the offensive

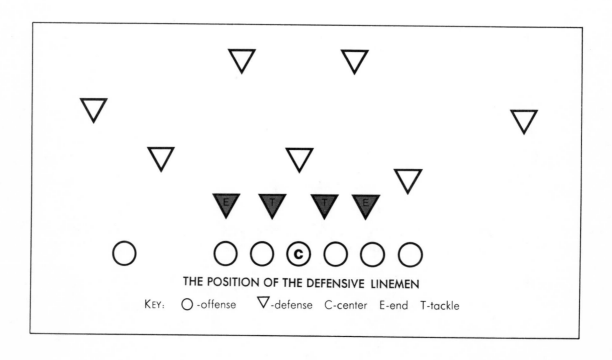

THE POSITION OF THE DEFENSIVE LINEMEN

KEY: ◯ -offense ▽ -defense C-center E-end T-tackle

40

linemen, trying to break into the offensive backfield to "sack" the quarterback or tackle a runner behind the line of scrimmage.

Before the defensive lineman can get into the backfield, he must get past the blocker. In this job the defensive lineman has one great advantage—he can use his hands while the blocker can't. He can throw the blocker out of the way if he's strong enough. More often, he will try to "get under" the offensive man's block, then hit or push him away with his forearm or hands. This technique aims to straighten the blocker up and throw him off balance. Then the defensive lineman is free to stop a runner or charge at the passer.

After making his first charge at the blocker, the lineman looks up to see where the play is going and to find the ball. Then he gets to the man with the ball by the fastest route. He must find the ball first, however. Otherwise he might charge blindly into the backfield only to discover that the ball carrier is already gone.

Unlike offensive players, who have assignments on each play and know what they are supposed to accomplish, a defensive lineman must decide on his own what to do on each play. Coaches teach their defensive lineman many tricks or "stunts" to help them get past the blockers. But above all, a good defensive lineman must have quick wits, a "nose" for the ball, and aggressiveness.

defensive strategy

Most of the famous football players are offensive players—great passing quarterbacks, shifty running backs, spectacular pass receivers. Until recently, the importance of defensive strategy and good defensive play wasn't recognized by the fans. But coaches have always felt that defense is the single most important aspect of football.

There are different defensive systems. But everyone agrees on the aims of the defense:

1. *To score.* This may seem surprising since the offense is the team with the ball.

But the defense can score in a number of ways. It can push the opponent back into the end zone to score a safety. It can intercept a pass or recover a fumble and run the ball for a touchdown.

2. *To get the ball.* Most coaches would say that this is always the defense's first job. Defensemen can force fumbles and interceptions. And they can hold the other team, forcing them either to punt or to give up the ball on downs.

3. *To prevent the easy touchdown.* This means that the defensive team must avoid simple mistakes. If a defensive back forgets which receiver to cover, for example, the offense can score suddenly and without really "earning" the touchdown. No matter how strong a defensive team is, it can't afford to give away touchdowns.

4. *To make the offense pay for every yard it gains.* The defense must make gaining ground hard and slow for the offense. If an offensive team can march down the field in only 6 or 7 plays, it will score often. But if it requires 20 plays to cover the same distance, it may make a mistake and lose the ball before it scores.

Coaches often divide defense into two parts. The first is called "forcing"—forcing the offense to hurry and to make mistakes. The defensive linemen are the center of the forcing unit, rushing into the offensive backfield on nearly every play in an effort to break up the offense's plans. The most important quality for defensive players who force the action is aggressiveness. They must be willing to do anything, within the rules, to get to the ball.

The other part of defense is "containment." The defensive backs are most important in holding the offense back, preventing long gains on any play. The linebackers are sometimes part of the containment unit and sometimes part of the forcing unit. Those working to contain the offense must be football-smart, recognizing early what the offensive play is and where it is going. Then they must work together to stop the play as close to the line of scrimmage as possible.

A smart defensive team always knows what the game situation is. They know the score, how much time is left, what down it is, and how many yards the offense needs. This knowledge often helps the defenders predict what kind of play will be coming next. For example, if the offensive team is behind by 14 points late in the game and has third down and ten yards to go, it will almost certainly pass because it needs the yards and the points desperately. In such a situation a defensive team would set up to defend against the pass and would put strong pressure on the passer. Football is a game of strength, but it is also a game of wits—the defense and the offense are always trying to outguess each other.

delay of game

A violation of the rule which states that a team must put the ball into play 30 seconds after the huddle has assembled—unless it calls a time-out. For delaying the game a team receives a five-yard penalty.

Denver Broncos

The quarterback knelt in the huddle and stared up at the white-shirted Broncos ringed around him. "Power sweep right," the quarterback said, looking at Floyd Little. "On two."

The Broncos trotted to the line of scrimmage, where the linemen of the San Francisco 49ers crouched. Floyd Little crouched behind the Bronco quarterback, hands on his knees. Only 5-foot-9, he was one of the smallest running backs in the NFL. But he was fast and could slip like an eel through the grasping hands of tacklers.

Denver running back Floyd Little almost loses his shirt in a tackle by Bengal linebacker Bill Bergey.

The quarterback shouted the signals—
"hut, hut." On the second "hut" he took the
snap from the center, spun, and handed off
the ball to Floyd, who sprinted toward the
sideline. Two big guards raced in front of
him, his blockers on this power-sweep play.
At the sideline Floyd tore by the San Francisco tacklers, who had gotten there an instant too late. Then Floyd flashed down the
sideline for an 80-yard touchdown run.

But the Broncos lost that 1970 game, 19–
14. During most of their seasons the Broncos
were losers. They were among the eight
teams that had made up the American Football League when it was formed in 1960.
During the AFL's lifetime—from 1960 to
1969—the Broncos won 39, lost 97 and
tied 3. Their best season was 1962, when
they won 7 and lost 7.

Their best players during those AFL
years were Lionel Taylor, a chunky pass
catcher who became the AFL's all-time pass
receiver; and Gene Mingo, a squat place-
kicker, who topped the AFL in scoring as a
rookie in 1960 and again in 1962.

Beginning in 1970, when the AFL
merged with the National Football League,
the Broncos played in the Western Division
of the American Football Conference.

In 1977, after several losing seasons, the
Broncos—under new coach Red Miller—
won the championship of the AFC. They
opposed the Dallas Cowboys in Super Bowl
XII and at first outplayed the Cowboys. But
the Cowboys soon poured through the Denver defense, called the Orange Crush, and
won, 27–10.

The Broncos play in Mile High Stadium,
which holds 63,500 people. The team colors
are orange, blue, and white.

Detroit Lions

"Just block a little, fellahs," drawled the
Texas-born quarterback, "and this old boy
will pass you to a championship."

The Detroit Lions, crouched in their huddle, grinned. They were used to the iron confidence of Bobby Layne. Time after time he
had thrown passes late in a game and turned
defeat into victory.

This game was for the 1953 NFL championship. The Lions were losing to Otto
Graham and his Cleveland Browns, 16–10.
There were only four minutes left. The ball
was on the 20-yard line, 80 yards from a
touchdown.

Bobby whipped three straight passes and
the Lions stood at midfield. On two running
plays the Lions smashed to the 33.

Standing in the huddle, end Jim Doran
told Bobby that he thought he could slip by
the Brown player who was guarding him.
"Okay," Bobby said, calling for a pass play.
Seconds later Bobby took the snap and faded
back. Doran raced at his man, faked a block,
then shot by him. Layne arched a high pass.
Doran sprinted under the ball, caught it at
the 10, and fled into the end zone.

Touchdown! Now the score was tied, 16–
16. Layne knelt to hold the ball for the
extra-point kick. Another tall Texan, Doak
Walker, was waiting to kick. Bobby grabbed
the ball, set it down. Doak Walker rammed
it straight over the crossbar. The Lions led,
17–16, as a loud roar filled the Detroit stadium. The Lions held the lead to win their
second successive NFL title.

That Lion team of the 1950s, featuring
the passing of Bobby Layne and the running
and kicking of Doak Walker, was the greatest in the first half-century of Detroit pro
football. A Detroit team, the Heralds, had
been one of the 13 original NFL teams when
the league began in 1920. But it soon
dropped out, as did several later Detroit
teams. In 1934 a Detroit radio station owner
purchased the NFL's Portsmouth, New
Hampshire, team and brought it to Detroit.
He renamed the team the Lions. (Detroit's
baseball team was called the Tigers.)

The Lions finished second in the NFL's
Western Division in 1934. Powered by the
runs of Ernie Nevers and the passes of Earl
"Dutch" Clark, they finished first in 1935
and beat the Giants, 26–7, for their first
NFL crown. They didn't win a second until

Quarterback Bobby Layne holds the ball for Doak Walker during a 1954 practice session at the Detroit Lions' training camp.

1952 when the team led by Layne and Walker beat the Browns, 17–7. The following year Layne's pass to Doran won another title. The Lions tried for their third successive title in 1954 but had their noses soundly smacked by the revengeful Browns, 56–10.

With Layne injured in 1955, the Lions slipped, but they bounced back dramatically in 1957. In a playoff game against the San Francisco 49ers for the Western Division title, the Lions were losing 27–3 in the third period. Then, with Tobin Rote as their new quarterback, the Lions roared back to win, 31–27. In the game for the NFL championship they blasted their old rivals, the Browns, 59–14, as Rote flipped four touchdown passes.

Through the remainder of the 1950s, the 1960s, and on into the 1970s the Lions were always a feared team. They had great defensive players, notably linebacker Joe Schmidt (later their coach), tackle Alex Karras, and defensive backs Dick "Night Train" Lane, Yale Lary, Jack Christiansen, and Lem

Barney. Runners such as Nick Pietrosante and receivers such as tight end Charlie Sanders were among the league's All-Stars. These Lions boosted the team to contending positions almost every season. After 1970 the Lions played in the tough "black-and-blue" Central Division of the NFC, and were blocked from reachings the playoffs and the Super Bowl by either Green Bay or Minnesota.

The Lions play at 80,368-seat Pontiac Metropolitan Stadium in Pontiac, Michigan, a suburb of Detroit. The team colors are Honolulu blue and silver.

draw play

A play that begins like a pass play, then turns into a running play. The blockers back up, as if to protect the passer, thus drawing the defensive men into the backfield. Then the quarterback keeps the ball, or one of the running backs takes the ball, and rushes by the tacklers straight down the middle of the field. A draw play works well against a team that has a strong pass rush.

drop-back pass

The most common type of pass play. The quarterback runs straight back from the line of scrimmage into a pocket formed by blockers and throws the ball from there. (*See also* play-action pass; roll-out pass.)

drop kick

A method of kicking the ball for a field-goal attempt or try-for-point. The ball is snapped to the kicker. He drops the ball as if to punt, but allows it to hit the ground before he kicks it.

The drop kick was an important weapon in early football. Jim Thorpe could drop-kick 40 or 50 yards accurately. But in the 1930s and 1940s, the shape of the football was changed. Its ends became more pointed. The new ball was easier to pass, but very difficult to drop-kick since its bounce was not reliable. Drop-kicking is still legal, but it is almost never used today.

LITTLE BOY BLUE

Mighty Army led Yale, 13–0, early in a 1929 game. Desperate, the Yale coach sent in a new quarterback—a sophomore named Albie Booth. Little Albie stood 5-foot-6 and weighed only 140 pounds. He looked like an elf next to his teammates.

To the Army players he soon looked like a blur as he slithered through the arms of tacklers for a touchdown. Then he drop-kicked the extra point. Later, he zigzagged for a second touchdown, kicking the extra point that put Yale ahead, 14–13. Then he dashed 65 yards for a third touchdown and booted another extra point, making Yale a surprise 21–13 winner.

In his blue Yale jersey, Albie became famous as Little Boy Blue, an All-America who proved conclusively that football is also a game for the little guy.

eligible receiver

A man who may legally catch a pass during a play from scrimmage. There are usually five eligible receivers: three backfield men and two ends. The fourth backfield man is the passer. The other five linemen may not catch a pass. In fact, they may not even run pass patterns to confuse the defense. They can't block more than three yards downfield on a pass play until the ball is thrown. If they do, their team is penalized for "ineligible receiver downfield."

end

On offense, an end is a player who lines up on the line of scrimmage outside the tackles. A split end lines up ten or more yards away from the tackle on his side. He is a pass receiver. The tight end lines up next to the tackle on his side. He may either catch passes or block. (*See* receiver; offensive lineman.)

On defense, the ends are the two outside linemen. They usually rush into the offensive backfield as soon as the ball is snapped. (*See* defensive lineman.)

end-around play

A play in which the end runs into his backfield, takes the ball on a surprise hand-off, and dashes around the opposite end. The end-around is one kind of reverse play. (*See* reverse.)

equipment

In a game that has as many collisions as football, protective equipment is important. There are rules in all football organizations that require all players to wear the basic equipment. In pro football the outfitting of a single player may cost $400 or more.

The basic pieces of equipment are:

The helmet. Players have worn some kind of headgear since the 1890s. Modern helmets are of two kinds. One has a network of cloth webs under the plastic shell. A blow on the head is cushioned when the webbing stretches. A newer air-suspension model has sacs of air and liquid that are even more effective than the webs in cushioning head blows. Head injuries are the most dangerous injuries in football. No one should play tackle football without a properly fitted helmet.

The face guard. Before the introduction of face guards as part of a player's gear, broken noses, loosened teeth, and black eyes were common. The face guard protects against all of these. It is attached to the helmet and comes in many variations. A simple double bar is favored by backfield players. Linemen and many defensive players prefer a cage type of mask that has two or three horizontal bars and one vertical bar down the center to protect the nose.

The shoulder pads. Modern pads are made of plastic with vinyl padding, and sometimes they have metal springs. The pads take the shock when a player blocks or tackles with his shoulders—and when he hits the ground. The pads are put on over the head and should fit properly.

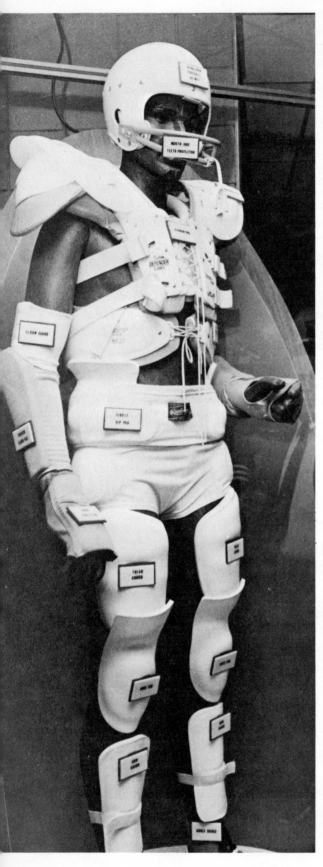

Shoes. Football shoes come in many varieties. Most have cleats to help grip the field, providing traction for fast starts, stops, and changes of direction. The type of shoe should match the playing surface. For example, shoes with long cleats may cause injuries on artificial turf because they tend to "catch" in it.

There are many other kinds of pads and equipment. These include a teeth protector, rib pad, sternum (breastbone) pad, elbow and forearm pads, hand protectors, hip pads, thigh guards, knee pads, and various kinds of ankle braces and protectors. No player wears all of this equipment, but most players wear some of it. In general, linemen wear more protective equipment and backfield players wear less.

For young players, the basic protective equipment is essential. Tackle football without equipment is dangerous. If a player does not have a helmet, shoulder pads, and face guard, he should stick to touch football.

extra point

The point scored on a try-for-point after a touchdown. (*See* scoring; try-for-point.)

F

fair catch

When the receiver of a punt sees that he is not likely to advance the ball after he catches it, he can decide to make a fair catch. He signals "fair catch" to the referee and his opponents by raising one hand in the air. He is then allowed to catch the ball without interference from the opposing team. If he catches the ball, play stops and the receiver's team takes possession of the ball at the spot where he caught the ball. The receiver who makes a fair catch may not run with the ball after he has caught it. If he drops the ball, he is considered to have fumbled and either team may recover it.

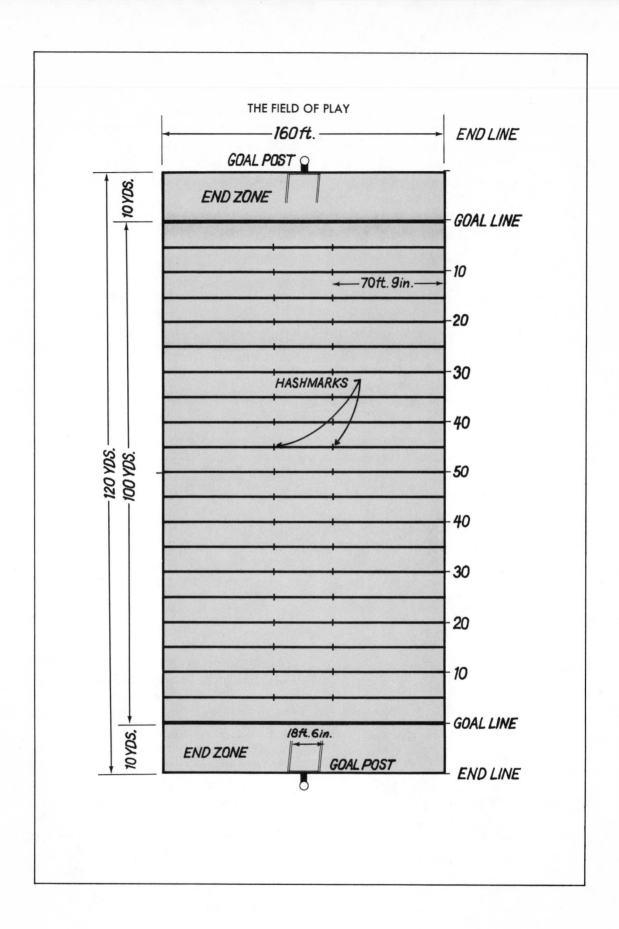

field goal

A scoring play worth three points. The ball is put down and kicked on a play from scrimmage. It must pass over the crossbar and between the uprights of the goal post. (*See* scoring.)

field of play

The standard football field is 120 yards long and 53⅓ yards (160 feet) wide. Each end zone is 10 yards deep, and the distance between the two goals is 100 yards. Lines cross the width of the field every 5 yards and are numbered from each goal from the 5- to the 50-yard line.

In football we say a team defends its own goal. The half of the field nearest its goal is called the team's territory. When a team moves the ball past the 50-yard line, it is going into the opponent's territory.

A goal post is placed on each end line, 10 yards behind the goal. The crossbar is 10 feet high (the same height as the basket in basketball). The uprights are 18½ feet apart in professional football and 23⅓ feet apart in high school and college football. So it's a little harder to kick a field goal or extra point in the pros.

The only other marks on the field are the hashmarks, which are short lines at right angles to the yard lines. These marks show where the ball is to be put into play if the previous play ended near a sideline or out of bounds. In pro football the hashmarks are near the middle of the field, so every play begins close to the middle. In college and high-school ball the hashmarks are 17⅔ yards from each sideline, dividing the width of the field into thirds. Before hashmarks were used, each play began where the last one ended, even if it was only 5 yards from the sideline. (*See* diagram on opposite page.)

flanker

A player in the offensive backfield who lines up far to the left or right of the offensive formation—out on the "flank." He usually serves as a pass receiver. (*See* receiver.)

football

The modern football is a "prolate spheroid." That means that it is pointed at both ends and is round through the middle. The regulation ball must be 11 to 11¼ inches long from point to point and 21¼ to 21½ inches in circumference at the middle. It should weigh between 14 and 15 ounces and be inflated with 12½ to 13½ pounds of air pressure. It should be covered with leather (although colleges allow the use of a rubber-covered ball).

In the early days of football, the ball was much less pointed and somewhat bigger around. This allowed players to drop-kick it. But throwing the ball was difficult. The ball was "streamlined" to its present shape so it would be easier to pass.

formations

One of the weapons the offense has in its battle with the defense is its formation—where the men are placed before play begins. The rules require that the offense has seven men on the line of scrimmage when the ball is snapped. The remaining four may line up anywhere on or behind the line.

Football teams have tried many formations. In the 1920s and '30s the most popular was the single-wing, in which the center could snap the ball directly to any of three men: the tailback (TB), the fullback (FB), or even the blocking back (BB). The wingback (WB) lined up several yards to one side, ready to take a pitchout or run out for

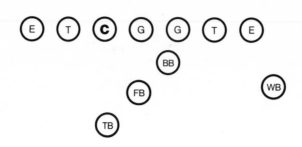

SINGLE-WING FORMATION

KEY: O-offense C-center E-end T-tackle G-guard BB-blocking back
FB-fullback WB-wingback TB-tailback

a pass. His position "on the wing" gave the formation its name. The single-wing was a good formation for running strong plays around one side of the defense. But the center's long snap could cause frequent fumbles. Also, the single-wing attack was not balanced. Since the team always lined up with more players on one side of the ball, it was difficult to run plays toward the other direction.

In the late 1930s college and pro teams began to experiment with the T-formation. The success of Stanford University and the Chicago Bears with the T soon made it popular around the country. By 1950 it was the standard offensive formation. Since then coaches have discovered many variations on

the T, but the basic idea has never changed.

The most important feature of the T is that the quarterback lines up directly behind the center and takes a short, direct snap. The ball is actually handed to him without traveling through the air.

The formation got its name from the way the three other backs originally lined up behind the quarterback. Directly behind the quarterback, at the top of the T, stood the fullback (FB), usually the biggest running back. On each side of the fullback stood the two halfbacks. They formed the top of the T. Often, one of them was a small, shifty runner and the other was a blocker who could run interference for a ball carrier or help protect the quarterback on pass plays.

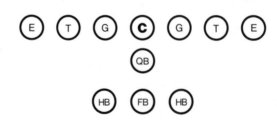

T-FORMATION

KEY: O-offense C-center E-end T-tackle G-guard QB-quarterback
HB-halfback FB-fullback

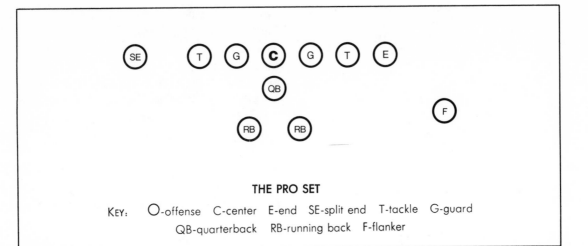

THE PRO SET

KEY: O-offense C-center E-end SE-split end T-tackle G-guard
QB-quarterback RB-running back F-flanker

The main pass receivers in the traditional T were the two ends.

The variation of the T that has been widely adopted by professional teams is sometimes called the "pro set." The quarterback is still directly behind the center. But the job of some of the other players has changed. One of the halfbacks has become a pass receiver. He is called a flanker (F) and lines up far off to one side of the rest of the backfield. One of the ends splits wide, usually on the opposite side of the field from the flanker. This split end (SE) is the other main pass receiver. The other end lines up close to the tackle on his side and is called the tight end (TE). He may be used either as a blocker or as a pass receiver.

In the T and all of its variations, the most important player is the quarterback. Even if the coach calls the plays from the sideline, the quarterback must call the signals for the snap of the ball and handle the ball on every play (except for punts). He is usually the passer and he must be able to handle the ball well in making hand-offs or pitching back lateral passes to his running backs.

forward pass

A pass that travels toward the line of scrimmage. If the pass is not completed, the ball is dead when it hits the ground. (*See also* lateral pass.)

front four

The defensive line—two tackles and two ends. (*See* defensive lineman.)

fullback

A member of the offensive backfield. The fullback in the standard T formation is usually the power runner who carries the ball on plays through the middle of the line. In earlier days there were one fullback and two halfbacks in the backfield, all of whom carried the ball on running plays. In modern formations there are usually only two running backs in the backfield and they are simply called "running backs." (*See* running back.)

Graham, Otto

The score was tied, 14–14. The Navy player punted the ball. North Carolina Pre-Flight's Otto Graham caught the ball near midfield. He dashed toward the sideline. Most of the blue-shirted Navy players swarmed after him. He was cornered. Otto spun and tossed a long lateral pass the width of the field. Standing all alone at the other sideline was a teammate who grabbed the ball and ran almost 50 yards for the touchdown.

The time was 1944, during World War II. Otto, an All-America tailback at Northwestern University, had come to North Carolina to study to be a Navy fighter pilot.

As it happened, Paul Brown, a former Ohio State coach, had been watching the game. Afterward he talked to Graham. Brown told him that a new pro football league would be set up at the end of the war. Brown was to coach one of the teams. It would be named after him—the Cleveland Browns. He wondered if Otto would be his T-formation quarterback.

Graham hesitated. "I've never been a T quarterback," he objected. At Northwestern he'd been a single-wing tailback.

"You can be a T quarterback," said Brown. "You know how to handle the ball."

In 1946, when the war was over, Otto became the T-formation quarterback for the Browns in the new All-America Football Conference. He threw soft passes that arched into the hands of receivers who ran toward the sideline. "If thrown perfectly," Otto said, "that sideline pass is impossible to knock down or intercept."

"He seems to pull the string on the ball and set it down nice and easy on the receiver's hands," said Paul Brown. In the four seasons from 1946 to 1949 the Browns won 52 of 58 games, as well as the league championship for each of those seasons.

In 1950 the Browns joined the old, established NFL. Some fans sneered. They maintained that Otto was a minor-league passer and the Browns were only the champions of a bush league. The Browns promptly proved them wrong. They won the NFL's Eastern title, then beat the Rams for the NFL championship. (*See* Cleveland Browns.)

The Browns won six straight Eastern titles from 1950 to 1955. Three times they won the world championship—in 1950, 1954,

Cleveland star Otto Graham picks up yards to help the Browns win the 1950 championship.

The Galloping Ghost, Red Grange, carries the ball for Illinois.

and 1955. After that last title, Otto retired. He had completed 55.7% of his passes, a percentage topped only by Bart Starr and Sammy Baugh. The Hall of Fame ranks Otto as the leading passer of all time.

Grange, Red

It was early fall in 1924. Thousands of fans had come to Champaign, Illinois, to celebrate the opening of the University of Illinois's new football stadium. Its team would be playing a strong squad from the University of Michigan.

Michigan kicked off. An Illinois player with the number 77 on his jersey caught the ball on the 5-yard line. He ran to the right, then cut back to the center of the field. The Michigan tacklers seemed to surround him. But Number 77 spun and faked his way past them, breaking into the clear. He ran 95 yards for a touchdown.

Number 77 was Red Grange. He was on his way to becoming one of the greatest running backs ever.

A few plays later, Michigan punted and Illinois took the ball on its 33-yard line. On the first play the ball went to Grange, who carried around right end. The Michigan tacklers didn't even touch him as Grange ran 67 yards for another score.

The next time Illinois got the ball, the 5-foot-11, 175-pound Grange ran through the Michigan line 56 yards for another touchdown. He seemed to have some magic power. The Illinois fans cheered themselves hoarse. When he got the ball again he ran for a fourth touchdown, this time for 44 yards. In four carries he had gained 262 yards and scored 24 points. It was probably the greatest display of ball carrying ever seen.

Grange scored a fifth touchdown later in the afternoon. And he did almost as well in other games for Illinois. After playing his last game as a senior in 1925, he signed a contract with the Chicago Bears. Not many people watched pro football in those days. But when they heard that Red Grange, the famous "Galloping Ghost," would be playing, they came by the thousands. In one pro game in New York, 20,000 fans were turned away because the stadium was already overflowing with 70,000 people. The disappointed fans nearly caused a riot—all because they wanted to see Red Grange. Grange was paid $30,000 for that one game, a fee that not even today's high-priced players have topped.

During his second season in pro football, Grange injured his knee. After that, he never ran quite as well with the ball. Although Red Grange never scored five touchdowns in another game, he was the most popular player of his day, and he certainly proved that pro football had enormous potential for drawing huge crowds of fans.

Grange quit as a player after the 1934 season and later became a famous voice on football telecasts.

Green Bay Packers

As the players huddled, their breath puffed out steamy white into the cold air, and an Arctic wind whipped at their faces. The temperature was 13 degrees below zero, and the frozen turf was hard as concrete. In the stands the spectators were numb from the wind and cold. Yet no one was leaving while the Green Bay Packers huddled around their quarterback, Bart Starr.

The Packers were behind, 17–14, in this 1967 championship game against the Dallas Cowboys. Though they stood just one yard away from a winning touchdown, there were only 13 seconds left to play. And this was fourth down—the Packers' last chance to score. If they failed, the clock would tick off the final seconds and the Packers would lose.

"They should kick a field goal!" said a fan. "They can't miss from only one yard away. A field goal would tie the game. And they could win in overtime."

But Vince Lombardi, coach of the Packers, ordered his team to go for a touchdown. If they made it, they would win the game and the championship. In the huddle, Bart Starr said he would carry the ball. "And we better make it!" he snapped.

Starr *hut-hutted* signals into the cold air, then took the ball from the center. The two lines smashed together. Guard Jerry Kramer rammed into a Cowboy lineman, knocking him down. Running behind Kramer, Starr saw a crack of daylight. He dived through the crack and into the end zone. A touchdown! The Packers had won the game and their 11th NFL championship.

That 1967 squad was perhaps the greatest of all Packer teams. The Packers had started in 1919, when a former Notre Dame running back—Earl "Curly" Lambeau—suggested to his boss at the Indian Packing Company in Green Bay that the company sponsor a team. The boss agreed to buy uniforms for a team to be called the Packers. The next year the Green Bay Packers paid $50 to join a year-old professional league, an organization that would soon be called the National Football League.

Curly was the team's coach and its flashy runner. The Packers won three straight NFL championships in 1929, 1930, and 1931. Lambeau retired as a player but he remained as coach, finding a spindly-legged runner to take his place as player. This new man's name was John McNally, but he called himself Johnny Blood. Blood swaggered into huddles, confident he could run for a touchdown whenever he had to. Once he told the Packer quarterback, "Just zoom the ball as far as you can." Johnny Blood raced to the end zone, leaped for the ball, and came down with three opponents piled on top of him. When the referee had untangled all the legs and arms in the heap, he found Johnny Blood at the bottom, gripping the ball for the winning touchdown.

In the 1930s the Packers had two quarterbacks who could zoom the ball—first, Arnie Herber and, later, Cecil Isbell. Then a lanky end came out of the University of Alabama

Bart Starr (15) crashes through for the winning touchdown after Jerry Kramer (64) takes care of the Cowboy opposition in the 1967 NFL championship game.

to join the team. He ran like a greyhound, leaped as though climbing stairs, and had fingers like flypaper. His name was Don Hutson.

The passing combination of Isbell to Hutson became as familiar to fans as ham and eggs. With Isbell passing to Hutson—and a pair of runners, Johnny Blood and Clarke Hinkle, smashing through lines—Curly Lambeau's Packers won NFL championships in 1936, 1939, and 1944. The 1944 championship was Lambeau's sixth and last.

Then followed many years of losing. The team was nearly always among the league's weakest. In 1958 the Packers won only one of 12 games.

A new coach—Vince Lombardi—was hired. Lombardi fixed his players with stern eyes, telling them, "Winning is the only thing."

Within two years the whip-cracking Lombardi watched his team turn from losers into winners. Two slashing runners, Paul Hornung and Jim Taylor, dashed for touchdowns. Bart Starr threw short, sharp passes to receivers Boyd Dowler and Max McGee. Huge pass rushers such as Willie Davis sacked the opposition's quarterbacks while quick backs such as Willie Wood and Herb Adderley intercepted passes. The Packers won NFL titles in 1961, 1962, 1965, 1966, and 1967. At the end of the 1966 season they won Super Bowl I, defeating Kansas City, 35–10, and they came back to win Super Bowl II by crushing Oakland, 33–14.

Then Lombardi retired as head coach. Starr, Taylor, Hornung and the other stars faded. So did the Packers. In 1970 they became part of the NFC's Central Division, which was dominated for its first half-dozen years by the Minnesota Vikings. But Packer fans kept on dreaming of one day seeing again in Green Bay championship seasons like those of Lambeau and Lombardi.

The Packers play in Lambeau Field, which is on Lombardi Avenue in Green Bay. They also play games in nearby Milwaukee at County Stadium. Lambeau Field seats 56,267; County Stadium, 55,896. The team colors are green and gold.

Greene, Joe

"I know a lot of eyes are watching me," Joe Greene said to his friend. "And I know why they're watching. They're watching to see how badly I'm playing."

Joe Greene trudged slowly toward the trainer's room, where a doctor was waiting to examine him. It was the fall of 1976. A pinched nerve in Joe's neck had caused his left arm to wither and lose its strength. "Right now," Joe said to his friend, "I'm in pain. I'm awkward, I'm slow. But I'll beat this. I've got to."

The strapping 6-foot-4, 275-pound Joe had been called Mean Joe Greene ever since his first NFL season in 1969. Joe, born in Temple, Texas, had played at North Texas State. His team was called the Mean Green. When Joe joined the Pittsburgh Steelers as a defensive tackle, sportswriters heard him talk about the "Mean Green." They thought he was talking about himself. Then one day he tackled quarterback Fran Tarkenton so hard that the crash was heard all the way up in the press box. The writers began to call him Mean Joe Greene.

Joe hated the nickname. "How would you like to be called Mean?" Joe often asked. "It makes you sound like you're something less than human."

But Joe *was* mean. He bowled over runners and he buried quarterbacks for a Steeler team that won two straight Super Bowl games—in January 1975 and 1976. (*See* Pittsburgh Steelers.) Then, suddenly, that pinched nerve—as painful as a continual toothache—slowed down Joe in the 1976 season. Opposing runners shot through his side of the line for long gains. The Super

Mean Joe Greene on the prowl.

Bowl champs lost four of their first five 1976 games.

Then doctors began to treat the pinched nerve, and gradually Joe's arm regained its strength. Again he stormed in on passers; again he cut down runners. The Steelers won nine straight games, capturing the championship of their division. But in the playoff game for the 1976 AFC championship, they were beaten by Oakland.

All the same, Joe was his old terrifying self once more. "Don't ever get Joe mad," Viking coach Bud Grant once said. "He'll murder someone." That kind of compliment made Joe frown, but it was also the reason why people kept calling him Mean Joe Greene.

guard

A member of the offensive line. There are two guards, and they line up on each side of the center. (*See* offensive lineman.)

Halas, George

Some men play football. Some coach football. Others own football teams. But very few men have done all three. George Halas not only did all three—he did them at the same time.

As a college player at the University of Illinois, Halas showed more determination than talent. He played end from 1914 to 1916 but never made much of an impression. During World War I, he served in the armed forces and played football for the Great Lakes Naval Training Station. Great Lakes played a marine team in the 1919 Rose Bowl, and in that game Halas was a star player. He caught two touchdown passes and set up a third score by intercepting a pass and running it back half the length of the field.

When he left the service, he looked for a way to make a living in sports. He couldn't play professional football because pro football didn't really exist yet. So he accepted an offer from the New York Yankee baseball team. He seemed to have great promise, but before his first season he injured his hip. He was sent down to the minor leagues and quit when the season was over.

Halas was not a great athlete. But he had a great idea. Why couldn't there be major-league football, he asked. For the rest of his life he devoted himself to creating professional major-league football. In 1920 he played for and coached a team sponsored by the Staley Starch factory in Decatur, Illinois. He entered the team in the American Professional Football Association (which would soon change its name to National Football League).

The next year Halas became the owner of the team and moved it to Chicago. Then he changed the team's name to the Chicago Bears. More than half a century later, Halas still owned the Bears, and he had become the father of the modern pro game. He had played for his team from 1920 to 1929. He had coached them for 40 years, finally retiring as coach in 1967. And the history of his team contained some of the high points of professional football.

In 1925 Halas hired Red Grange, the great running back from the University of Illinois, offering him thousands of dollars. The gamble paid off handsomely both for the Bears and for football in general. Suddenly thousands were turning out to see

George Halas (right) with football's first superstar—Red Grange.

Grange run with the ball, not only in Chicago but all around the country. Halas's later stars included running back/tackle Bronko Nagurski, quarterback Sid Luckman, linebacker Dick Butkus, running back Gale Sayers, and many others.

Halas also contributed to changes in football strategy. In the 1940 NFL championship game, the Bears produced a new version of the T formation. The Washington Redskins were caught off guard, and the Bears won, 73–0. Within ten years, all but a few of the pro and college teams in the country were using a T like the Bears'.

By the mid-1970s, Halas had retired from active management of the Bears, but he was still chairman of the board. More than that, he was still "Papa Bear," the man who personified the history of pro football from its beginning to the present.

(*See also* Chicago Bears.)

halfback

A player in the offensive backfield. In the standard T formation there are a quarterback, a fullback, and two halfbacks. In the modern pro set, one halfback is called the flanker and is usually a pass receiver. The fullback and the other halfback are called running backs. (*See* running back; receiver.)

half time

The break between the first and second halves of a football game has become a time for show business. Down on the field, marching bands perform. Up in the stadium, fans in cheering sections do card tricks, each one holding up a card that becomes part of a giant pattern or picture. On special occasions thousands of balloons are sent into the sky or fireworks are set off.

Probably the biggest half-time noise occurs every year on band day in Ann Arbor, Michigan. Between halves of a University of Michigan game, more than 50 bands march onto the field and play together—nearly 4,000 musicians performing at one time.

Many half-time shows include pageants with costumed performers and a narration spoken over the public address system. Not all events are planned, though. During half time at a 1976 Brigham Young University game in Provo, Utah, a student skydiver floated in over the stadium from a nearby mountain to make a perfect landing on the field.

hall of fame

The Professional Football Hall of Fame is in Canton, Ohio, where the first successful professional league was organized in 1920. (*See* National Football League.) The Hall of Fame honors great players, coaches, and team owners. A selection board meets each year to elect new members. So far, nearly a hundred men have been elected for their contributions to the game. They include many of the people whose names appear in this book. The Professional Hall of Fame also has a research library, and a museum devoted to early football.

A college football hall of fame is being planned at Rutgers University in New Jersey, where the first college game was played in 1869.

hang time

The time that elapses between the moment a punter kicks the ball and the moment a receiver catches it. A good punter kicks the ball high as well as far, trying to achieve a hang time of four and a half seconds or more. These few seconds give the kicker's teammates time to race downfield and tackle the receiver before he can run back the ball.

Harris, Franco

Would he do it again? That was the question most of the 81,000 fans jammed into the New Orleans stadium for Super Bowl IX were asking. Would the Pittsburgh Steelers dare to rush Franco Harris a third straight time against the ferocious Minnesota Viking defensive line?

It was early in the third period of this 1975 game. The Steelers, having scored on a safety, led the Vikings, 2–0. The Pittsburgh team had just pounced on a Viking fumble 30 yards from the goal line. On the first play, quarterback Terry Bradshaw gave the ball to running back Rocky Bleier, who was stopped for no gain.

On the next play Bradshaw handed off to Franco Harris. Franco burst through the Vikings and streaked 24 yards to the 6-yard line. On the next play Bradshaw again gave the ball to Harris, who was tackled for a 3-yard loss.

In the huddle Bradshaw called for Franco to carry the ball a third straight time, even though he knew the Purple People Eaters, the Vikings' famous defensive line, would be bunching up to stop Franco.

Bradshaw called the signals. He took the ball, spun, and handed it to Franco. The hulking Franco dashed around end like a runaway express train, outstripped the Purple People Eaters, and bolted into the end zone. It was the first touchdown of the game. Moments later the Steelers led, 9–0, and they went on to win the Super Bowl and their first National Football League championship, 16–6. Franco had carried the ball for 158 yards—a Super Bowl record.

The Steelers won a second straight NFL championship in 1976 when they beat the Cowboys in Super Bowl X, 21–17. (*See*

Pittsburgh Steelers.) In Pittsburgh, fans waved green, white, and red flags whenever Franco streaked for long gains. The Steeler fans called themselves "Franco's Italian Army." Franco's mother is Italian. His father is a black American. The soft-spoken, bearded Franco (32) always waved back.

Big Franco—he stands 6-3, weighs 230 pounds, and runs like a sprinter—has been rushing for records ever since his first NFL season. Coming from Penn State, he joined the Steelers in 1972 and became the seventh player in NFL history to gain more than a thousand yards as a rookie. In fact, in four of his first five NFL seasons, Franco gained at least a thousand yards. (A thousand yards is as important to a rusher as a .300 batting average is to a baseball hitter.)

"Trying to stop Franco," an NFL lineman once said, "is like trying to stop an army."

hashmarks

Short marks at right angles to the yard lines. They mark where the ball is to be put into play if the previous play ended near the sideline or out of bounds. (*See* field of play.)

holding

A violation of the rule that an offensive player may not use his hands or arms to hold a defensive player in any way. Defensive players, however, may use their hands to hold, shove, or push off an offensive player. But they are not allowed to punch, grab an opponent's face mask, or use unnecessary roughness. A defensive player may be called for "illegal use of the hands" but not for holding. (*See* penalty.)

Houston Oilers

The sixth quarter—yes, the *sixth* quarter!— of the game began. Most games end after four quarters. But this game had been tied, 17-17, at the end of four quarters. A 15-minute sudden-death overtime quarter began. The first team to score would be the sudden-death winner. But after the fifth quarter the score was still tied, 17-17. Because the sky over the Houston stadium was now dark, bright lights shone down on the sixth quarter of a game that had begun in bright sunlight.

The Dallas Texans (later the Kansas City Chiefs) and the Houston Oilers were battling for the 1962 American Football League championship. The Oiler quarterback was George Blanda, a graying veteran who threw passes and kicked field goals. The Oilers— aiming for a third straight AFL championship—had at first fallen behind, 17-0. Then Blanda had passed for one touchdown, kicked a field goal, and steered the team to another touchdown. He had kicked the extra point that tied the score, 17-17.

Early in the sixth quarter the Texans, led

by quarterback Len Dawson, fought to the Oiler 18-yard line. Rain was beginning to pelt both the players and the huddled spectators. On fourth down a rookie, Tommy Brooker, ran onto the field to try for the field goal that could win the game.

"Don't worry, baby," the brash Tommy said to a teammate, "it's all over."

Moments later it *was* all over. Brooker rammed the ball between the uprights. The Texans were 20–17 victors in what was, up to then, pro football's longest game. The official clock had ticked for 1 hour, 17 minutes, and 54 seconds.

The Oilers' two-year reign over the young AFL had ended. Houston never won another AFL championship despite the high scoring of George Blanda and the jarring tackles of linebacker George Webster.

In 1970 the Oilers joined the NFL with other AFL teams. They played in the Central Division of the American Football Conference. In 1975, under coach Bum Phillips, the Oilers began to rise again. They won 10 and lost 4, finishing third in the division.

The Oilers play in the Astrodome, the first covered stadium to be built. It holds 50,000. The team's colors are scarlet, Columbia blue, and white.

Don Hutson, Alabama All-America

Hutson, Don

The lanky Green Bay end sped toward the goal line with a defensive back close behind him. At the goal line the lanky end suddenly stopped, and wrapped a skinny arm around the goal post. Then he spun in a full circle, stuck up his free hand and caught the pass for a touchdown.

That lanky end was Don Hutson. He was the first of the shifty, pass-catching ends. By 1945 he had set enough records to fill this column. Most of those records have since been wiped off the books by all the star pass catchers who followed Don. But today's receivers play in games where as many as 20 or 30 passes are often thrown. In Don's day, big runners smashed for most of the yardage.

A quarterback who threw 10 passes was "a passing fool."

Green Bay Packer passers looked for Don because he was nearly always open. Opposing teams put two, and even three, men on him, yet Don ducked away to catch passes. "He's incredible," said one coach. "The man can run three ways at once."

Don grew up in Pine Bluff, Arkansas, and entered the University of Alabama in 1931. Another end on the Alabama team was a hulking fellow named Paul "Bear" Bryant, later a famous coach. (*See* Alabama, University of.) No one could stick with the string-bean Don, who stood 6-foot-1, weighed 180 pounds, and could run 100 yards at the Olympic speed of 9.7 seconds. Hutson could make everyone think he was going one way, then quickly dart off in another direction.

With strong-armed "Dixie" Howell to arch passes at Don, Alabama went to the Rose Bowl at the end of the 1934 season. Near the end of the first half, Stanford led, 7–0. Desperate, Alabama tried a long pass. Hutson caught the ball in the end zone to tie the game, 7–7. In the second half Howell completed five of six passes to Hutson. Alabama won, 29–13.

In 1935, Don joined the Packers. He was paid $300 a game, a high salary for the time. On the first play of his first game he seemed to be loping down the field. A Bear defensive back took his eyes off Hutson for a second to check on another receiver. When the Bear looked back to locate Don, the Packer end was gone. Hutson caught a pass for an 87-yard touchdown that won the game, 7–0.

The fabulous scoring career of Don Hutson had begun. He caught passes for touchdowns. He flashed for touchdowns on end-around plays. He kicked extra points, and on defense he played safety.

The fans called Don the Alabama Antelope, and said he had three speeds: fast, faster, and fastest. He snared passes from Arnie Herber and later from Cecil Isbell as the Packers won three world championships from 1935 to 1945. (*See* Green Bay Packers.) In 11 years he led the league five times in scoring. And eight times he led the league in pass catching—still a record. All told, he caught 488 passes for 7,991 yards. That record has since been surpassed, but his record of catching 99 touchdown passes still stands. In fact, no one is even close. As someone once wrote of lanky Don Hutson, he was *the* end.

I formation

A modern formation in which three backs line up one behind the other for the snap of the ball.

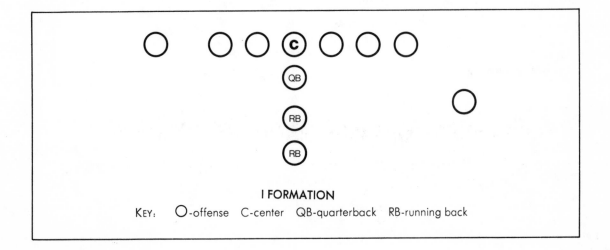

I FORMATION
KEY: O-offense   C-center   QB-quarterback   RB-running back

illegal procedure

See penalty.

illegal use of hands

See holding; penalty.

incomplete pass

Any forward pass that hits the ground before being caught, or any pass thrown out of bounds. As soon as the forward pass is ruled incomplete the ball is dead and play is stopped. The next play begins at the original line of scrimmage. If a pass is a lateral (traveling backward or sideways instead of forward), the ball is *not* dead when it hits the ground and may be recovered by either team.

independent

A college team that belongs to no conference. (*See* conferences.)

intentional grounding

When a quarterback is being chased behind his line of scrimmage, he may try to throw a pass. If the pass is incomplete, the next play will begin at the original line of scrimmage. But if the quarterback is tackled, the team will lose yardage.

Some quarterbacks throw the ball at the ground so the team won't lose yardage. But if the referee believes that the quarterback had no receiver in mind and was just trying to throw an incomplete, he will call "intentional grounding." Intentional grounding calls for a 5-yard penalty in college football and a 15-yard penalty in pro football.

interception

The catching of a pass by a player on the defensive team. The ball immediately belongs to the defensive team; the man who intercepted the pass may run the ball back.

interference

The rules say that a defensive player may not touch a pass receiver while the pass is in the air. (The only exception is when both receiver and defender are leaping for the ball.) If the defender pushes or trips the receiver or gets in his way while the ball is in the air, the referee calls pass interference. The ball is placed on the spot where the violation occurred. On a long pass, this penalty may be 30 yards or more—one of the most damaging in football. So defensive backs should be careful not to interfere with receivers.

Ivy League

Ivy League: *See* conferences.

Kansas City Chiefs

On a January morning in 1970—only a few days before Super Bowl IV—the newspaper headlines announced:

DAWSON LINKED TO GAMBLERS

Len Dawson was quarterback for the Kansas City Chiefs. A reporter claimed that Dawson was suspected of knowing gamblers who bet on games. Fans began to wonder. Had Lenny given tips to the gamblers to help them win their bets? Such a thing would be against NFL rules. "We have no evidence that Len Dawson is guilty," said NFL commissioner Pete Rozelle.

But when Len Dawson walked into the Super Bowl to face the Minnesota Vikings, he knew that millions of eyes were on him. If he played poorly, people would say he had played badly on purpose to enable the gamblers to win their bets. Lenny *had* to play well.

The game began. In his cool, soft-voiced way, Lenny called plays. The Chiefs marched into Viking territory. Jan Stenerud booted a field goal. The Chiefs led, 3–0. Stenerud kicked two more field goals for a 9–0 lead.

Len Dawson kept the Chiefs moving. He threw short passes, then handed off the ball to his cannonball of a running back, little Mike Garrett. The Chiefs won, 23–7. Len Dawson was voted the game's best player. He had proved he was no crook.

The Kansas City Chiefs started their ca-reer in 1960 as the Dallas Texans, one of the eight teams that formed the new American Football League. Their coach was Hank Stram. In 1962 the Texans battled the Houston Oilers for the AFL championship. (*See* Houston Oilers.) After almost 18 minutes of sudden-death overtime, Len Dawson held the ball and Tommy Brooker kicked a 25-yard field goal to beat Houston, 20–17. That ended what had been the longest game in pro football history up to that time.

In 1963 the team moved to Kansas City and was renamed the Chiefs. Each year the Chiefs were among the most feared teams in the AFL. Dawson flipped passes to the rabbit-quick Abner Haynes. And big backs Jack Spikes and Curt McClinton knifed through their opponents' lines. In 1966 the Chiefs won another AFL championship, smothering Buffalo, 31–7, in the title game. As the AFL champs, they met the NFL champs, the Green Bay Packers, in Super Bowl I. The Packers, who had too many great players for Hank Stram and his Chiefs, won Super Bowl I, 35–10.

Stram, Dawson, and the Chiefs bounced back to win the last AFL championship in 1969. And in Super Bowl IV, Lenny Dawson coolly ignored that cloud over his head and steered the Chiefs to victory over the NFL's Vikings.

In 1970 the AFL and NFL merged. The Chiefs joined the AFC's Western Division. They won the division title in 1971. In the first round of the playoffs they met the Miami Dolphins. Three times the Chiefs led as Dawson flipped passes to flanker Otis Taylor, and burly running back Ed Podolak shot through holes in the line. But each time the Dolphins stormed back to tie the game, knotting it at 24–24 late in the fourth period. But with only 31 seconds remaining, the Chiefs moved to just 31 yards from the goal line. A field goal would win the game for them. Kicker Jan Stenerud trotted onto the field. Usually he never missed at this distance. And Len Dawson held the ball, just as he had done for Tommy Brooker eight years earlier. But Stenerud's kick curved wide of the goal posts. Red-faced, he walked off the field under the eyes of 45,000 unhappy fans in the Kansas City stadium.

The game went into a 15-minute sudden-death overtime. The first team to score would be the winner. In that overtime period Stenerud tried another field goal, this one from the 42-yard line. But the kick was blocked by Miami linebacker Nick Buoniconti. The weary teams dragged into a second overtime. Finally Miami's left-footed kicker, Garo Yepremian, kicked a 37-yard field goal that won the game, 27–24, and ended—after 82 minutes and 40 seconds—the longest NFL game ever.

During the next few years, the Chiefs slipped in the standings as Dawson, Podo-

lak, and Taylor slowed down. Hank Stram, the Chiefs' first coach, was replaced.

The Chiefs play in Arrowhead Stadium, Kansas City, Missouri, which seats 78,000. The team's colors are red and gold.

key

Defensive players must react quickly when the offense attacks. Coaches teach defensive players to "key" on a particular player. For example, a linebacker may key on the other team's quarterback. If the quarterback drops back with the ball, the linebacker moves backward to cover a pass receiver. If the quarterback turns to hand the ball off, the

Kansas City's Len Dawson is tackled by a Viking after handing off to Mike Garrett (21) during Super Bowl IV (1970).

linebacker charges in toward the ball carrier. Professional players on defense sometimes have three or more keys on a single play.

kicking

In other forms of football, such as soccer, the ball is moved down the field by kicking, and every player must learn various kicking techniques. But in American football, kicking is used only to attempt to score (field goal or point-after-touchdown) or to turn possession of the ball over to the other team (kickoff or punt). The odd fact is that most football players never get a chance to kick the ball at all.

Punting: A team usually punts the ball when it faces fourth down and is not within 30 or 40 yards of the goal. Punting is a difficult and important specialty. The punter must often kick the ball out of danger when his team is in trouble, and he must kick while being rushed by opposing linemen. If he punts poorly, or if the kick is blocked, the opposition is usually in good position to score.

The punter usually stands about 12 yards behind the line of scrimmage and receives a direct snap from the center. He must get the ball off within a few seconds—without the time or space for a running start. Most coaches teach a punter to take one and a half steps before kicking the ball. If the punter is right-footed, he receives the snap while standing with his left foot slightly ahead of his right. He takes a short step forward with his right foot, then a full step with his left. As he lands on his left foot, his right leg begins to swing through for the kick. He drops the ball so that the big toe of his right foot strikes it slightly ahead of his body and about a foot off the ground. The ball is dropped so that it points slightly to the left. It should come off the foot in a spiral, spinning counterclockwise. A spiral kick meets less air resistance than a tumbling end-over-end kick, so it travels farther.

Learning to punt reliably and accurately takes lots of practice to get the timing and the contact with the ball just right. Professional punters often kick 50 to 100 balls in practice. Their aim is to make their technique so automatic that they can kick the same way every time. Beginners kick mostly for distance. But pro punters also kick for height, so that their teammates will have plenty of time to get downfield and be ready to tackle the punt returner the moment he touches the ball. (*See* hang time.)

Place-kicking: This requires a slightly different form. On kickoffs, the ball is set up on a tee and the kicker can take his time. His aim is to get plenty of power behind the ball. He may take eight running steps or more to

Place-kicking: traditional style   *soccer style*

gain momentum before booting the ball. Pro kickoff specialists can kick 60 or 70 yards almost every time.

In place-kicking for a field goal or point-after-touchdown, accuracy is usually more important than power. The ball must travel over the crossbar of the goal posts. (The posts are 18½ feet apart in professional football and 23½ feet apart in the amateur game.) The field-goal kicker must get his kick off quickly. Like the punter, he is rushed by the opposition.

There are two popular styles of place-kicking for field goals. In the traditional style, the kicker lines up two steps behind the point where the ball will be placed down, his left foot ahead of his right. As soon as the ball is snapped, he takes one step with his right foot, then plants his left foot about six inches to the left of the ball and six inches behind it. His toe points directly at the target. The kicking foot swings directly into the ball, toe first, hitting the ball below its midpoint. The farther below the midpoint, the higher the kick will go.

In the modern soccer-style kick, which was made popular by Europeans who played soccer before coming to American football, the kicker approaches the ball from an angle. A right-footed kicker stands to the left of the ball and behind it. As he approaches the ball, he plants his left foot to the left of the ball, pointing in the direction of his approach. The kicking leg swings on a diagonal to the body from back and out to front and in. The foot strikes the ball with the instep—the side of the foot along the side of the big toe. Soccer kickers claim they are more accurate because the kicking surface of the instep is wider than the kicking surface of the toe.

kicking game

Even though kicking is a specialty that few players ever have to master, all players and coaches soon realize that the kicking game is a very important part of football. A team with a great punter and a great place-kicker can keep its opponents far back in their own territory and can score even when unable to move the ball across the goal for a touchdown.

When a team lines up to punt, it has two

important missions. First, it must protect the punter to make sure the kick is not blocked. Then it must hurry downfield to tackle the receiver. A team is often told to block aggressively for three or four counts, then to "release" and head for the punt returner. At the moment the returner touches the ball, the men on the kicking team become tacklers and the men on the receiving team become blockers for their ball carrier.

The team receiving a punt also has two missions. The first is to block the kick or at least hurry the punter. (They must be careful not to run into the punter—a penalty for roughing the kicker allows his team to keep the ball.) Their second goal is to clear a path for the punt returner. In one common formation, the linemen on the receiving team "peel back" as soon as the kick is in the air,

forming a wall of blockers along one sideline. The receiver is supposed to carry the ball between the sideline and the blockers.

Kicking plays (punts and kickoffs) are more open than plays from scrimmage. Players are spread over a wide area and most tackling and blocking take place in the open field, so the individual skills of each player are most important. These skills include thinking quickly, adjusting to new situations, and performing open-field blocks or tackles effectively. Mistakes can be costly since there are often no teammates close enough to help out.

Players must also take special care to protect themselves on kicking plays. The "special teams" that go onto the field in kicking situations in pro football are sometimes called "suicide squads" because injuries are

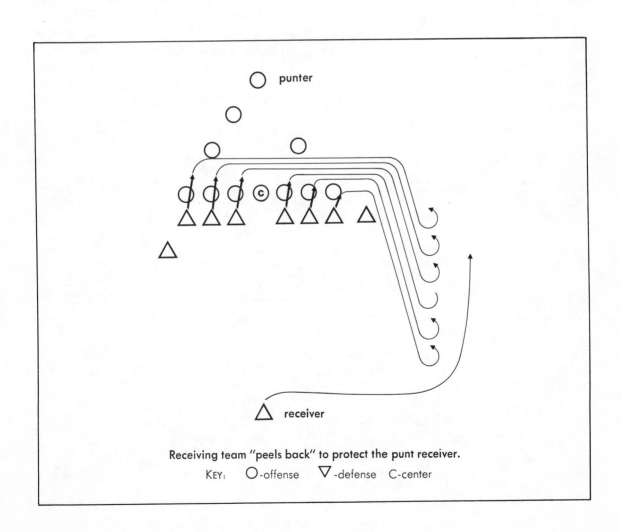

Receiving team "peels back" to protect the punt receiver.

KEY: O-offense ▽-defense C-center

so common. This is because players run into each other at high speed and because an opponent may come at a player from any direction. Officials are particularly alert for violations. Players should be careful not to block from the back (clip) or make illegal blindside tackles. On punts, the receiving team players must remember that they can use their hands only until the returner touches the ball. Then they become blockers and can't use their hands without risking a penalty.

kicking records

See records.

Kramer, Jerry

The Green Bay Packer linemen moved quickly toward the line of scrimmage. The linemen of the Dallas Cowboys were already there, crouching.

Packer guard Jerry Kramer took his three-point stance. He knew how much depended on him—the winning or the losing of a game and a championship.

The Cowboys led the Packers, 17–14, in this struggle for the 1967 NFL title. The Packers were only a yard away from a touchdown. But just 13 seconds remained, time for only one play. In the huddle quarterback Bart Starr had called for a plunge by himself —through a hole that Jerry Kramer would have to blast open.

Starr barked the signals. As the ball was snapped, Jerry threw a "wedge block." His 6-foot-3, 245-pound body drove like a green arrow between two white-shirted Cowboys. Starr, running right behind, wiggled through the hole opened up by Jerry's thrust. He squirmed into the end zone for the touchdown that won the game and the NFL championship. (*See* Green Bay Packers.) Jerry's

THE FOOTBALL FIELD THAT SHRANK

In 1932 the Chicago Bears played the Portsmouth Spartans for the NFL championship. On the day of the game, the temperature was 30 degrees below zero. So the game was played indoors in Chicago Stadium. A circus had just left. The players wrinkled their noses when they came onto the field, for the aroma of elephants still lingered in the steamy air.

The field had to be shrunk 20 yards in length and 10 yards in width to fit between the stadium walls. So that the players wouldn't smash into the walls, the ball was put into play at least 10 yards from the sideline when the previous play ended out of bounds. (Until then the rule had been that the ball had to be put into play almost smack on the sideline.)

The Bears won, 9–0, and everyone liked the 10-yard rule, because it meant that teams could run left or right instead of only one way. The NFL kept the rule, but it moved its championship games back outdoors, where they have stayed.

block was later called "the most famous block in football history."

Jerry Kramer soon became the most famous offensive linemen ever. He wrote a book about that block and about being a Packer. The book was called *Instant Replay*. The title was chosen because Kramer's block was seen again and again on television, thanks to TV's instant-replay machine.

Kramer grew up in Jordan, Montana, where he fished in the summer and skied in the winter. After attending the University of Idaho, he joined the Packers in 1958. It was Jerry, as one of the guards, who led the Packers' most famous play—the Green Bay Power Sweep.

On the power sweep, the two guards pulled out of the line to lead a charge toward the left or right. The ball carrier followed the wave of blockers. When they executed the play, Jerry and his fellow guard knocked down would-be tacklers the way a bowling ball topples pins.

Jerry played during the Packers' glory years of the 1960s. The team won five championships and the first two Super Bowls. In 1968 he retired. He had succeeded in doing what no other guard had ever done. He was the first offensive lineman to become famous.

Krause, Paul

The Redskins' rookie defensive back rubbed his moist hands nervously. The Cleveland

Paul Krause intercepts a pass for the Washington Redskins.

quarterback was calling out the signals in this 1964 game. The rookie was nervous because he knew the quarterback was going to pass. He hoped that the pass wouldn't go over his head for a touchdown.

The ball was snapped. The Cleveland pass receiver—the great Paul Warfield—raced down the sideline. The rookie raced after him. Then he turned and saw the ball spiraling downward. The rookie leaped, intercepted the pass, and ran the ball back 40 yards before he was tackled.

The rookie was Paul Krause. And that interception was the first in his NFL career. As the free safety—first for the Redskins, later for the Minnesota Vikings—Paul was his team's "center fielder." He roamed the deep secondary to knock down or intercept long passes. If Paul didn't get a hand on a pass, it might well end up as a touchdown for the opposing team.

"My job," he said, "is to stop the long bomb. If I don't, everyone in the stadium sees me chasing a receiver into the end zone. They know I gave up six points."

Oddly, Paul was once a real center fielder. He roamed center field for the University of Iowa baseball team. Big-league teams wanted to sign him. But he injured a shoulder and could no longer throw hard enough to be a big-leaguer.

For the University of Iowa football team, he played on offense and defense. He caught passes as a wide receiver, and he intercepted passes as a free safety. In 1964 he joined the Washington Redskins, where he set an NFL

Krause as a Minnesota Viking.

record that still stands. He intercepted passes in seven straight games. And in that 1964 season he led the league with 12 interceptions. In 1968 he was traded to the Vikings. For five straight seasons from 1971 to 1975 he was picked as the NFC's best free safety.

By 1976 he had intercepted 76 passes. The record for the most passes intercepted in a career was 79, achieved by Emlen Tunnell, a former Giant and Packer. "That's my goal, topping that record," Paul said. It was a goal he seemed almost certain to reach.

lateral pass

A pass that travels sideways (toward the sideline) or backward (away from the line of scrimmage). If a lateral pass is not caught, the ball is free and can be recovered by either team. (*See also* forward pass.)

linebacker

Many coaches believe that the linebackers are the most important players on the defensive team. One of the linebackers is often defensive captain and calls the signals for his unit. But whether or not he is captain, a good linebacker can be as important to a defense as a good quarterback is to the offense.

In the usual professional defense, there

are three linebackers. The two outside linebackers play behind and outside the defensive ends. The middle linebacker plays about a yard behind the line of scrimmage—between the tackles and directly in front of the other team's center. (*See* diagram.)

Linebackers must be able to act both as linemen and as defensive backs. They have important assignments on every kind of offensive play—runs through the middle, sweeps and end runs, and passes. Coaches often choose their quickest and most talented big men for the linebacker position.

On most plays, linebackers do not rush into the offensive backfield. Since they don't usually rush, they take a two-point stance, standing slightly crouched with their weight on the balls of their feet, ready to move rapidly in any direction. They have three major jobs. The first is to stop any runner who comes through their part of the line. Since on most running plays one of the offensive linemen is assigned to block the linebacker, the linebacker must first get free of the blocker, then charge toward the ball carrier to stop him.

The linebacker's second responsibility is to pursue any ball carrier who runs around end. (The middle linebacker pursues in either direction.) The linebacker's aim is to force the runner outside—toward the sideline—and keep him from making his turn downfield. In order to accomplish this, the linebacker must think quickly to recognize the play, and move just as quickly on his feet to stop it.

The third responsibility for linebackers is to defend against short passes, usually within about ten yards of the line of scrimmage. The outside linebackers must watch the sideline areas on their side of the field and the middle linebackers must cover the short zone in the middle of the field.

So the linebacker must be big and tough enough to tackle bruising running backs on running plays, strong enough to make open-field tackles, and fast enough to cover quick pass receivers. Most important, the linebacker must think quickly enough to know

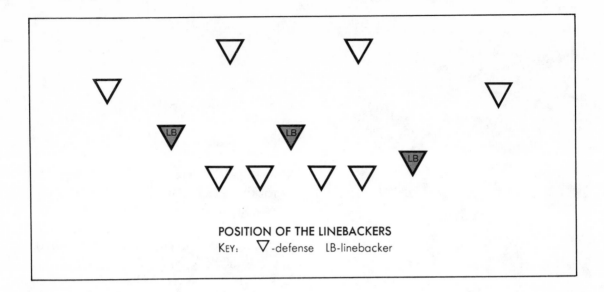

POSITION OF THE LINEBACKERS
KEY: ▽ -defense LB-linebacker

what to do and when to do it on each play. In short, he must be the all-around defensive player.

lineman

See defensive lineman; offensive lineman.

line of scrimmage

An imaginary line that runs from sideline to sideline through the middle of the ball. The offensive team must line up behind this line with at least seven men within a yard of it. They are said to be "on the line." The defense lines up on the other side of the line. No one may cross the line of scrimmage until the ball is snapped, and any forward pass must be thrown from behind the line of scrimmage.

Lombardi, Vince

The stocky, bull-necked coach strode into the team's training room. At least 20 players were lined up, waiting to have bruised arms and legs taped.

"What's this?" the coach roared. "You've got to play with these small hurts, you know."

The embarrassed players fled from the training room. The next day only two lined up for treatment. One was A. D. Williams, whose foot was swollen. "How're you feeling?" the coach asked in his booming voice. Williams hopped out of the room. "I feel better already, Coach," he stammered.

Vince Lombardi had just taken over as head coach of the Green Bay Packers, a once-proud NFL team that had lost every game but one in the 1958 season. With his gruff, whip-cracking approach, Lombardi began to rebuild the team. He assembled a backfield that included passer Bart Starr and running backs Jim Taylor and Paul Hornung. He built an offensive line of blockers led by Jim Ringo and Jerry Kramer. For defense he forged a solid wall secured by linebacker Ray Nitschke and lineman Henry Jordan. Of Lombardi's grueling practices, Jordan once said, "He treats us all the same. Like dogs."

Lombardi told his players that football was a simple game of blocking, tackling, and running. "The team that wins," he shouted at them, "is the team that tackles better, blocks better, and runs to daylight."

Lombardi had learned how to block and

Coach Vince Lombardi

tackle at Fordham University. There he had been one of "the Seven Blocks of Granite," a line that held a mighty University of Pittsburgh team to scoreless ties in 1936 and 1937. Later, Lombardi coached a New Jersey high-school team that roared through 32 games without a defeat. In the 1950s he was an assistant coach of the New York Giants and helped them to win the 1956 NFL title.

In 1959 Lombardi took over the demoralized Packers. By 1960 the team was champion of the West. The Packers won the NFL title in 1961, 1962, 1965, 1966, and 1967. (*See* Green Bay Packers.) They also won the first two Super Bowls, in 1967 and 1968. After retiring as Packer coach, Vince Lombardi came back to coach the Washington Redskins for a year. In 1970 he died of cancer.

Today the Lombardi Trophy is given in his memory to the winner of the Super Bowl. That trophy is a memorial to the man who once said, "Winning isn't everything. It's the only thing."

Los Angeles Rams

The Rams' quarterback, Pat Haden, knifed into the pile of players at the goal line. The Minnesota Vikings flung him backward. When the players untangled, the referee signaled no touchdown for the Rams.

It was fourth down, with just inches to go for the touchdown. The score was tied, 0–0, in this game between the Rams and the Vikings for the 1976 NFC championship. The winner would go to the Super Bowl.

While more than 47,000 shivering fans watched in the frigid Minnesota stadium, Ram coach Chuck Knox decided to try for a field goal. His kicker, Tom Dempsey, had seldom been known to miss when he was this close to the goal posts.

The Ram center snapped the ball toward Dempsey, who was waiting to kick the ball. Dempsey swung his foot. The ball shot upward. A Viking lineman stuck up a hand and blocked the ball. Another Viking player scooped it up and ran 90 yards for a touchdown. Just like that, the Vikings had turned the tables on the Rams. They had scored to take the lead, 7–0.

The Rams seemed stunned by that blocked kick. They didn't score until the third period. By then it was too late. The Vikings won, 24–13, to go to the 1977 Super Bowl.

The Rams went home to moan about how often they had come close to the Super Bowl—only to stumble over the last hurdle. The Rams had never been inside a Super Bowl. And they hadn't won an NFL championship since 1951.

The Rams began as the Cleveland Rams, joining the NFL in 1937. They didn't have a winning season until 1945, when rookie quarterback Bob Waterfield became a Ram. Waterfield, who had the slick hands of a magician pulling a rabbit out of a hat, mastered the "bootleg" play. He faked giving the ball to a running back. Then he hid the ball behind his leg. Opponents tackled the empty-handed running back while Waterfield slipped around end for a touchdown.

With Waterfield tossing and running for touchdowns, the Rams won the 1945 Western championship. Then they played the Eastern champs, the Washington Redskins, for the NFL title. When the Redskins' Sammy Baugh tossed a pass from the end zone, the ball hit the goal post. According to a rule of the time—a rule which was later changed—the Rams were given two points for a safety. That freak play won the game for the Rams, 15–14, and gave them their first NFL championship.

In 1946 the team moved to Los Angeles, becoming the first NFL team on the West Coast. By 1950 Waterfield was throwing passes to sticky-fingered receivers Elroy "Crazy Legs" Hirsch and Tom Fears. And big Ram runners such as Tank Younger were blasting through enemy lines. The Rams won the Western title in 1950. But in the championship game—played against the Cleveland Browns—they lost on a last-minute field goal, 30–28. The next season the Rams beat the Browns, 24–17, for their second NFL crown. In 1955, with Norm Van Brocklin now their strong-armed passer, the Rams again were kings of the West, but they were bowled over in the title game, 38–14, by Otto Graham and his Browns.

Ram quarterback Pat Haden (11) is tackled by Viking defensive end Mark Mullaney in the 1976 NFC championship game.

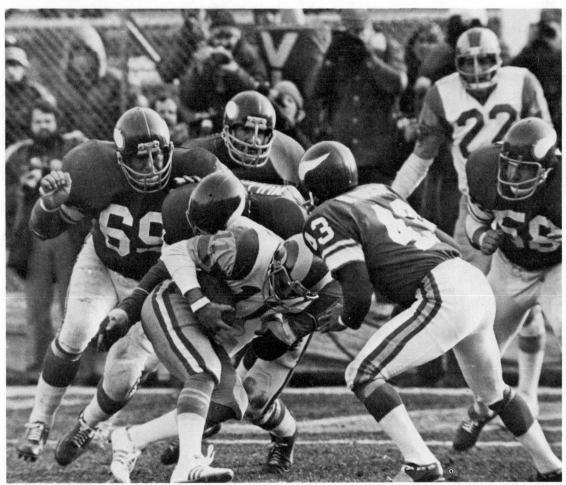

In the 1960s the Rams built a huge defensive front wall. That front wall rushed at passers, doing its best to bury them. It became famous as the first "Fearsome Foursome." The 270-pound Deacon Jones and 280-pound Merlin Olsen usually led the rush. But the Rams didn't score enough points to win a division title until Roman Gabriel, a black-haired 6-foot-4 passer, began to connect with receivers such as Jack Snow and Bernie Casey. Although the Rams won division titles in both 1967 and 1968, each time they were beaten in the playoffs so they did not succeed in getting to the Super Bowl.

In 1970, when the team became part of the NFC's Western Division, Gabriel's arm began to ache and the Rams faltered on their drives for touchdowns. Then in 1973 a new coach, Chuck Knox, arrived. He built up a new Fearsome Foursome around the veteran Merlin Olsen. And he found new running backs Larry McCutcheon, Jim Bertelsen, and John Cappelletti to bull through holes for long gains. The Rams won the Western Division title four straight years from 1973 to 1976. But each year another team pushed them out of the playoffs before they could reach the Super Bowl—the one place where they had never played.

The Rams play in Los Angeles Memorial Coliseum, which seats 91,038 and is the NFL's biggest stadium. The team colors are royal blue, gold, and white.

RED'S FIFTH DOWN

Some 30,000 fans watching a 1940 Dartmouth-Cornell game thought they were seeing the upset of the year. Cornell was unbeaten while Dartmouth had lost four games. But Dartmouth was leading, 3–0, with only a minute left.

Cornell, however, had the ball only six yards away from the winning touchdown. On first down Cornell drove to the 3, on second down to the 1, on third down to the 1-foot line.

Cornell called time-out to stop the clock, since there were only nine seconds left. Referee Red Friesell stepped off a five-yard penalty against Cornell for taking too many time-outs. On fourth down Cornell threw a pass that was batted down.

Dartmouth fans cheered. Their team had held. But on the field Red Friesell had become confused. He said it was now fourth down. On what was actually the fifth down, Cornell threw a pass for a touchdown. Cornell thought it had won, 7–3.

But the next day Dartmouth officials showed movies of the game to Friesell. He agreed that he had made a mistake. And Cornell graciously conceded the victory to Dartmouth, 3–0. There have been many upsets in football, but none as strange as Dartmouth's "fifth-down" upset of Cornell.

man-in-motion

After the offensive team has lined up and before the ball is snapped, one offensive man may be moving—either toward the sideline or away from the line of scrimmage. He is called the man-in-motion. He may not move toward the line of scrimmage until the ball is snapped. If he does, he will be called for illegal procedure. (*See* diagram below.)

man-to-man defense

A type of pass defense in which each defensive back covers a particular receiver. (*See also* zone defense.)

Miami Dolphins

Bob Griese studied the Minnesota Viking defense. The Vikings were standing with their backs to the goal line. Griese, crouching over the center, *hut-hutted* signals. He took the ball, spun, and slammed it into the belly of Larry Csonka. The hulking Csonka pushed into the end zone. Moments later Garo Yepremian kicked the extra point. Although this 1974 Super Bowl game was only a few minutes old, the Dolphins already led Fran Tarkenton's Vikings, 7–0.

A minute later the Dolphins were driving toward the goal line again. On the 1-yard line Griese took the ball. This time he gave it to Csonka's pal, Jim Kiick. Kiick dived over for another touchdown. The Dolphins led, 14–0.

The Miami defense—it proudly called itself the No-Name Defense—trotted onto the field. It threw back the Viking runners and batted down Tarkenton's passes. At the finish of the game, the Dolphins walked off the field 24–7 winners. They were Super Bowl champions for the second year in a row.

Coach Don Shula had assembled a well-balanced Dolphin team with a brick-wall defense and a steamrolling offense. Miami fans

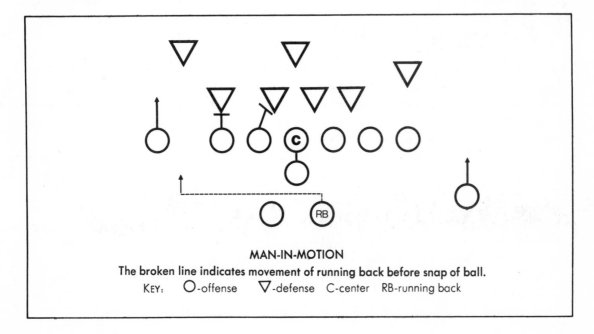

MAN-IN-MOTION
The broken line indicates movement of running back before snap of ball.
KEY: O-offense ▽-defense C-center RB-running back

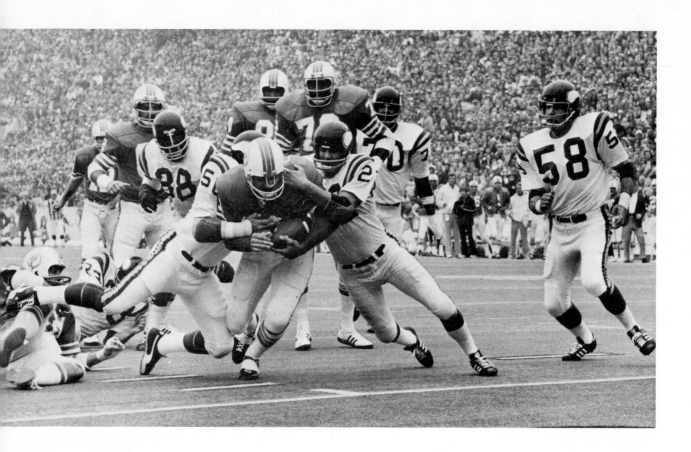

were delighted, for they had suffered through years when the Dolphins seemed to be doormats for other teams to step over. The Dolphins had joined the American Football League in 1966 as the AFL's first "expansion" team. The eight original AFL teams fed the baby Dolphins their worst players. From 1966 to 1969, the last year of the AFL, the Dolphins lost more games than they won.

But gradually they began to acquire some good players: a young blond quarterback from Purdue named Bob Griese; a stocky linebacker named Nick Buoniconti; a slender pass receiver, Paul Warfield; and two line-smashing runners. The runners called themselves "Butch Cassidy and the Sundance Kid," but they were listed on the roster as Larry Csonka and Jim Kiick.

In 1970, after the merger of the AFL and NFL, the Dolphins lined up in the AFC's Eastern Division. They finished second with a 10–4 record and qualified, as the "wild card" team, for the playoffs. (*See* wild card

team.) Oakland beat the Dolphins in the opening round. But coach Shula now had a team with playoff experience. "We'll make it to the Super Bowl one day," he predicted.

And they did the next season. Though they lost to the Cowboys, 24–3, in the 1972 Super Bowl, they returned the very next year and beat Washington, 14–7. And at the end of the 1973 season they went to their third successive Super Bowl game, where they rolled over the Vikings by that 24–7 score.

In 1974, however, they failed to squeeze by Oakland in the opening round of the playoffs, losing 28–26. In 1975 Csonka, Kiick, and Warfield jumped to the new—and short-lived—World Football League. (*See* World Football League.) The Baltimore Colts took over as the number one team in the AFC East in 1975 and 1976, but Miami fans firmly believed that the Dolphins would rise again.

The Dolphins play in the Orange Bowl at Miami, a stadium which seats 80,045. The Dolphin colors are aqua and orange.

(left) Miami fullback Larry Csonka (39) plows through the Minnesota defense to score the first touchdown of the 1974 Super Bowl.

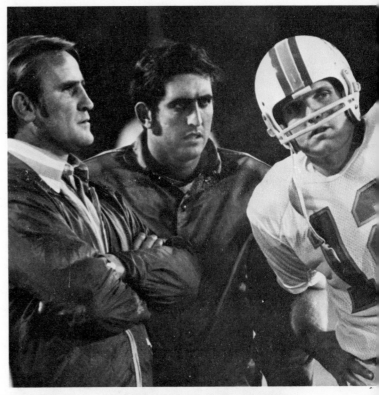

(right) Dolphin coach Don Shula with backup quarterback George Mira (center) and Bob Griese (right).

(below) Quarterback Griese drops back to hurl a pass in the 1973 Super Bowl. Larry Csonka (39) blocks.

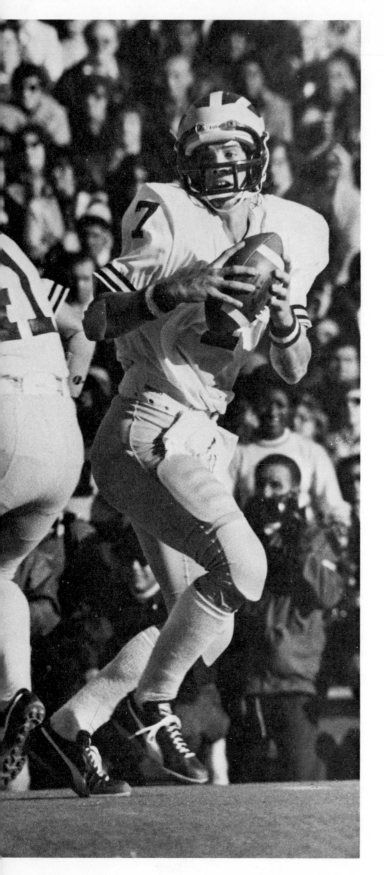

Michigan, University of

The biggest game on the University of Michigan schedule every year is the Ohio State game, the last of the season. In 1975 the Michigan Wolverines had been held to a tie against Ohio State, and had lost a chance to go to the Rose Bowl. Instead, Ohio State went for the fourth year in a row.

In 1976 Michigan was favored to be the best team in the nation. But in the middle of the season, it lost a game to Purdue. Ohio State, as usual, won all of its Big Ten games. So when the Wolverines traveled into enemy Ohio for the last game of 1976, they knew that they had to beat Ohio State just to tie for the Big Ten title. And, of course, the winner would go to the Rose Bowl.

The first half of the game was scoreless. But Michigan coach Bo Schembechler and his quarterback, Rick Leach, weren't discouraged. On the first play of the second half, Leach ran for 9 yards. Seconds later, running back Rob Lytle ran for 15. The Wolverines were on the march. They scored three touchdowns and won, 22–0. Powerful Ohio State suffered its first scoreless game in 12 years.

In the late 1970s, the Wolverines ran away from the rest of the Big Ten, winning three straight titles in 1977–79. But they weren't as successful at the Rose Bowl, losing three in a row, one to Washington State and two to Southern Cal.

The football tradition at Michigan is a long and distinguished one. From 1901 to 1905 the early Wolverine teams under coach Fielding "Hurry Up" Yost won 29 games in a row, were held to a tie on the next one, then won 26 more. The 1901 team, which scored 516 points and allowed none to its opponents, won the first Rose Bowl game on New Year's Day, 1902, defeating Stanford, 49–0.

Michigan quarterback Rick Leach about to get off a pass.

Forty-six years later, under another great coach, Fritz Crisler, Michigan returned to the Rose Bowl and beat the same team by the same score. (Stanford finally got even in 1972, nipping an undefeated Michigan squad by a single point.)

The University of Michigan is in Ann Arbor, about 50 miles from Detroit. Michigan Stadium is the largest college stadium in the country, seating 101,000. The school colors are maize and blue.

Minnesota Vikings

The Los Angeles Rams' quarterback smashed into the mountain of bodies at the goal line. One of the purple-shirted Minnesota Vikings shoved him backward. The big crowd in the Viking stadium let out a happy roar.

The Viking defense—named the Purple People Eaters—had halted the Rams at the goal line. It was now fourth down. The score was 0–0 early in this game for the 1976 championship of the National Football Conference.

The Rams decided to go for a field goal. The ball was snapped back to the 17-yard line. The Rams' Tom Dempsey stepped forward and booted it. Suddenly a Viking rusher swerved out from the right side, stuck up a hand, and blocked the kick. The ball tumbled crazily toward the sideline. It was scooped up by another Viking, Bobby Bryant, who scooted all the way down the sideline, 90 yards, for a touchdown. The Vikings led, 7–0.

That blocked kick shook the Rams. The Vikings won, 24–13, to enter their third Super Bowl in four years. So far the Vikings had never won a Super Bowl game. But Viking quarterback Fran Tarkenton vowed, "We'll win this one!"

They didn't, however. In Super Bowl XI the Oakland Raiders crushed the Vikings, 32–14. All told, the Vikings had now played in four Super Bowls—more than any other team—and they had lost all of them.

The Vikings had joined the NFL in 1961 as a new "expansion" team. The majority of the players had been sent to the Vikings by teams that didn't want them. "Most of them are a bunch of soreheads who couldn't get along with their coaches," wrote one reporter. One exception was a quarterback, fresh out of college, named Fran Tarkenton. In his first regular-season game, the rookie quarterback completed 17 of 23 passes. The Vikings won the first game they had ever played in the NFL, shocking the Chicago Bears, 37–13.

But the seasons from 1961 to 1967 were mainly losing ones for the Vikings. Tarkenton was traded away. Then the team got a

The Vikings' Bobby Bryant (20) intercepts a pass intended for the Rams' Ron Jessie (81) in the 1976 NFC championship game.

85

new coach—Bud Grant. In 1969 the Vikings topped their division and won the NFL championship. They met the Kansas City Chiefs in Super Bowl IV. There the Chiefs beat the Vikings, 23–7.

In 1970, after the AFL-NFL merger, the Vikings joined the Central Division of the

Viking Chuck Foreman (44) blasts through the line for yardage.

NFC. Grant had built a terrifying defense led by such Purple People Eaters as 260-pound Alan Page and 270-pound Carl Eller. In 1972 Fran Tarkenton came back to rejoin the offense, and during the next several years he had some good receivers, such as Gene Washington, to throw to. Big running backs—notably Dave Osborn and Chuck Foreman—blasted through lines for yardage, while kicker Fred Cox was on his way to becoming an all-time high scorer.

The Vikings won the Central Division title every year except one from 1970 through 1976. During that time they won 75 of 98 regular-season games, and they took the NFC title in 1973, 1974, and 1976. But that "big one"—a victory in the Super Bowl—always slipped through their fingers.

The Vikings play in Metropolitan Stadium in Bloomington, Minnesota, a short ride from Minneapolis and St. Paul. The stadium holds 48,446. The team's colors—purple, white, and gold—gave the Viking defensive unit its name: the Purple People Eaters.

Nagurski, Bronko

Doc Spears, the coach of the University of Minnesota football team, was driving his car through the Minnesota farm country one summer day. He noticed a big, square-shouldered young man plowing a field. Spears was always looking for strong young football players. So he stopped the car and asked the young man for directions to the next town. "When he picked up the plow with one hand and pointed out the direction with it, I knew I had a player," Spears recalled.

Bronko Nagurski was the boy's name. Since he came from the land of Paul Bunyan, where people were used to tall stories, no one really believes he pointed with the plow. But Doc Spears did find a great football player. Nagurski became one of the strongest and fiercest running backs and linemen ever seen in the game. Playing for the University of Minnesota from 1927 to 1929, he was picked on every All-America team. He was so good that some judges picked him for his work as a defensive tackle and others picked him as a running back.

Bronko's opponents couldn't agree either. Some said the worst experience in the world was to be tackled by Nagurski. The others thought it was even more terrible to try to tackle *him*. Nagurski seemed so strong that he was his own blocker when he ran with the ball.

In 1930 the 6-foot-2, 230-pound Bronko joined the Chicago Bears and played with them until 1937. In one game he made a mistake on defense and allowed the other team to score. He was almost in tears. When the Bears got the ball again, the Bronk asked to carry it. He wanted to make up for his mistake. On the next play he ran straight through the enemy line. Although he was tackled by six different men, not one of them could bring him down. He didn't stop running until he reached the end zone 65 yards away.

On defense, Nagurski sometimes blocked the ball carrier instead of tackling him. But what a block he threw! He seemed to explode into the poor runner, and usually knocked him five yards up the field. The runner was lucky if he didn't fumble.

Bronko Nagurski had never played football before his arrival at the University of Minnesota.

In 1943 the Bears were short of players because many were in the armed forces, fighting in World War II. Nagurski came back to his old team and helped them to win the NFL championship that year. He was now 35 years old, but as strong as ever. That season he astounded younger players by averaging 5.3 yards a carry.

After his football days, Nagurski became a professional wrestler. Then he retired to northern Minnesota. He is still remembered there as a real-life Paul Bunyan—even if he didn't really point with a plow.

Namath, Joe

"I'm sure there's an empty feeling in New York today," said the Jet official. "Joe meant so much to the city."

He was talking about "Broadway Joe" Namath. Early in the spring of 1977, after 12 years of thrilling the fans with his passing on the field, Joe Namath had been released by the Jets.

No football player was ever more colorful than Joe Namath. Fans either loved him or hated him. He seemed arrogant, boastful, and vain. He wore his hair long at a time when most athletes cropped their hair short. He admitted that he stayed up all night having fun with friends before a big game. And his frequent appearances at Broadway night clubs in New York City earned him his famous nickname.

But Broadway Joe could get away with his colorful antics because the fans loved the way his strong right arm hurled passes that led to Jet victories. Even opposing players said that no passer threw with the quickness and the accuracy of Broadway Joe.

As a passer, Joe's greatest moments may have been at the 1968 AFL championship game. Despite Joe's two touchdown passes, the Jets were losing, 23–20, to the Raiders in the final period. The ball was 68 yards from the touchdown the Jets needed to win the game and go to the Super Bowl.

Joe streaked a pass to flanker George Sauer for 10 yards. He threw to lanky end Don Maynard for a 52-yard gain. And then he zipped his third straight completion into the hands of the diving Maynard for a touchdown. The roar of more than 60,000 New Yorkers filled Shea Stadium, for those three lightninglike strikes won the game, 27–23, and sent the AFL champion Jets winging into the Super Bowl.

This was the third Super Bowl battle between the best team of the American Football League and the best of the National Football League. NFL fans had been calling the AFL a minor league. In the first two Super Bowl battles, the NFL team had won easily, and the Baltimore Colts were favored to win Super Bowl III by 18 points. But before the game Joe stood up in front of hundreds of people and said, with a grin, "I think we'll win it. I guarantee it."

And win it the Jets did, by a 16–7 score. Joe completed 17 of 28 passes and was picked as the game's most valuable player. "Now," he crowed, "no one can call the AFL a minor league."

Many believed that Joe made the AFL a major league. Born in Beaver Falls, Pennsylvania, he had been an All-America passer at the University of Alabama. In the early 1960s AFL teams often played their games in front of crowds containing no more than 5,000 spectators. Jet owner Sonny Werblin thought that an exciting passer like Joe could attract more fans. In 1965 he signed Namath to a three-year, $425,000 contract. Joe's salary was the most money paid up to that time to a pro football player. As a result Namath became the center of a good deal of attention, and football fans began to look at the new AFL with more respect.

Twice, during the next few years, Joe led the AFL in passing, even though he was hobbled by damaged knees. Then came the great victory in the 1969 Super Bowl—a victory that Joe had predicted.

By the 1970s, however, Joe's knees ached so agonizingly that he often watched games from the sideline or from a hospital bed. And in 1977 he finally said good-by to the Jets. But New Yorkers would always remember him as the cocky scamp who "guaranteed" victory in the 1969 Super Bowl.

National Football Conference (NFC)

One of the National Football League's two conferences. The other is the American Football Conference (AFC). The NFC was established in 1970 when the National Football League and the American Football League merged. Thirteen of the 16 NFL teams formed the NFC (the other three joined the AFC). The NFC, like the AFC, is divided into three divisions—Eastern, Central and Western. Each year the NFC champion meets the champion of the AFC in the Super Bowl. (*See* National Football League; Super Bowl.)

National Football League (NFL)

A tall Indian leaned against the fender of a car. Around him a number of other men sipped beer and mopped their sweaty foreheads on a hot day in September 1920. These dozen or so men, sitting in an auto showroom in Canton, Ohio, were about to organize an association that would one day become the National Football League.

The Indian's name was Jim Thorpe. He was the most famous football player in America. An All-America runner in college, he was now the fearsome halfback for the Canton (Ohio) Bulldogs.

There were hundreds of pro teams like the Bulldogs scattered in towns and cities across the United States. Ever since 1892, when Pudge Heffelfinger was paid $500 to play for a Pennsylvania team, town football teams had hired players. Most of these teams played in parks before a few hundred people; some battled on sandlots. But the owners of these early pro football teams yearned to have a big league like baseball with teams playing in big-city stadiums before large crowds. Eleven owners had come here to Canton to form such a league.

The owners called the league the American Professional Football Association. Eventually, 13 teams paid $100 each to be members. As a way of getting newspaper coverage, the league appointed the famous Jim Thorpe as its president. The original 13 teams included George Halas's Decatur (Illinois) Staleys, the Chicago Cardinals, and the Dayton (Ohio) Triangles. Of the original 13, only two still exist—but with new names. The Decatur Staleys are now the Chicago Bears; the Chicago Cardinals are now the St. Louis Cardinals.

During the new league's first season in 1920, the teams played without a formal schedule and there were no league standings. Thus no team won the league championship.

Attendance at games was sparse. The league seemed about to collapse. But it managed to struggle into a 1921 season, joined by a team from Green Bay called the Packers. That year the Staleys won the league's first championship. In 1922 the league was renamed the National Football League, though most of the teams were located in the Midwest.

During the 1920s, the league expanded to as many as 22 teams. Some were in big cities —New York, Detroit, and Kansas City— but most of them were in places such as Portsmouth, New Hampshire, and Duluth, Minnesota. Players were traded for $100. Profits were as small as $23, the total net one season for the Bears.

Sports fans still looked on pro football as

minor league, though they were wild about college football. Sometimes as many as 100,000 spectators crowded into stadiums to watch such All-Americas as Illinois' Red Grange. Then in 1925, Grange, "the Galloping Ghost," joined the Chicago Bears. College fans suddenly flocked to see him run against the pros. In ten games the Bears earned $50,000. "Grange," said one owner, "proved that pro football could make money."

But the depression of the 1930s brought new problems. With so many people out of work, fans didn't have money to buy tickets. Teams began dropping out of the NFL. By 1933 the league had shrunk to eight teams. It split into two divisions—East and West. To make extra money, the East and West champions met in a post-season game for the 1933 NFL championship. The winner was the Bears, who beat the Giants by the close score of 23–21.

During the 1930s and through the World War II years of the 1940s, that NFL championship game attracted bigger and bigger crowds. It became known as "the world series" of football.

By 1946 professional teams were drawing as many as 50,000 to season games. In the East there were the Boston Yanks, the New York Giants, the Philadelphia Eagles, the Pittsburgh Steelers, and the Washington Redskins. In the West there were the Chicago Bears, the Chicago Cardinals, the Detroit Lions, the Green Bay Packers, and the Los Angeles Rams.

Seeing the huge NFL crowds, a group of rich men organized a new league—the All-America Football Conference. Among its stronger teams were Cleveland, San Francisco, and Baltimore. Salaries of the best players—Bobby Layne, Otto Graham, Doak Walker, Charlie Trippi, and others—soared as the leagues thrust money at players in order to get the best ones. One of the highest paid was Charlie Trippi, a halfback who received $25,000 a year from the Cardinals for being part of their "Million Dollar Backfield."

Some of the AAFC teams went broke,

Carl Brumbaugh of the Chicago Bears manages to get by the Giants' Ken Strong during the 1933 NFL championship game.

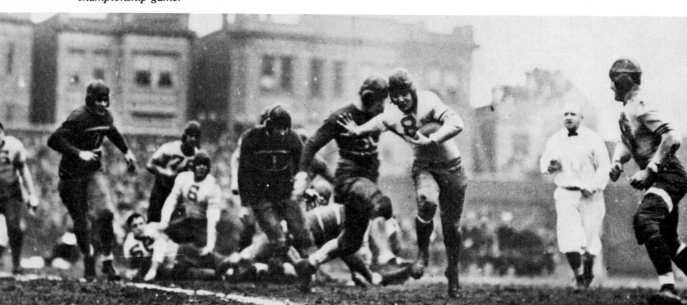

Television brought millions of new fans to pro football during the fifties and sixties.

and in 1950 the league collapsed. Three of its best teams—the Cleveland Browns, the San Francisco 49ers, and the Baltimore Colts—joined the NFL. (The Colts soon disappeared, but in 1953 the Dallas Texans moved to Baltimore and were renamed the Colts.)

Television attracted millions of new fans to pro football. NFL attendance rose from two million in 1950 to almost five million by the early 1960s. Again a group of wealthy men decided to get a share of the pro football profits. In 1960 they formed the American Football League. It had eight teams—Boston, Buffalo, Dallas, Denver, Houston, Los Angeles, New York, and Oakland. Once more, salaries jumped as the two leagues fought for the best players. The bidding seemed to hit a peak when the New York Jets paid more than $400,000 for three years to a rookie named Joe Namath from the University of Alabama.

The young NFL commissioner, Alvin (Pete) Rozelle, began to talk with AFL owners. In 1966 the two leagues signed a peace treaty. The NFL champion would meet the AFL champion in a post-season game for the world's championship of pro football. The game was called the Super Bowl. In 1970 the two leagues merged. The new NFL was divided into an American Football Conference and a National Football Conference. A playoff system was set up. Each season the ten teams with the best records enter a playoff. The playoffs end with two teams pitted against each other in the Super Bowl.

Today the 28 NFL teams draw more than 14 million spectators to their games. A star such as Ken Stabler earns more in a season —over $200,000—than all the 13 original NFL teams were worth in 1920. A team such as the Bears, valued at $100 then, is worth at least $15 million now.

The 28 teams in the NFL are:

AMERICAN FOOTBALL
CONFERENCE

Eastern Division
Baltimore Colts
Buffalo Bills
Miami Dolphins
New England Patriots
New York Jets

Central Division
Cincinnati Bengals
Cleveland Browns
Houston Oilers
Pittsburgh Steelers

Western Division
Denver Broncos
Kansas City Chiefs
Oakland Raiders
San Diego Chargers
Seattle Seahawks

NATIONAL FOOTBALL
CONFERENCE

Eastern Division
Dallas Cowboys
New York Giants
Philadelphia Eagles
St. Louis Cardinals
Washington Redskins

Central Division
Chicago Bears
Detroit Lions
Green Bay Packers
Minnesota Vikings
Tampa Bay Buccaneers

Western Division
Atlanta Falcons
Los Angeles Rams
New Orleans Saints
San Francisco Forty-Niners

Nebraska, University of

In 1975 the Cornhuskers of the University of Nebraska were invited to play in Hawaii. Some 7,000 Nebraska fans made reservations for the trip, flooding the airline offices and threatening a traffic jam at the Honolulu airport.

The Cornhuskers are worth supporting. In the 1960s, under coach Bob Devaney, they were one of the most powerful teams in college football. In 1970 they won the national championship. But they sneaked in by the back door, claiming the title only when the two favorites were upset in post-season bowl games. Not everyone believed Nebraska really deserved the honor.

So in 1971 Nebraska fans were looking for proof that the team really was number one. The Cornhuskers won all their games. But so did their rival, the University of Oklahoma. The two teams finally met on Thanksgiving Day. Football fans across the country watched on television to find out which of the teams was really number one.

It was one of the most exciting games ever played. First one team went ahead, then the other. Late in the fourth quarter, Oklahoma took a 31–28 lead. Then Nebraska got the ball on its 26-yard line with seven minutes left to play.

Led by quarterback Jerry Tagge, Nebraska marched methodically down the field, closer and closer to the Oklahoma goal. Finally, on the 11th play of the series, running back Jeff Kinney drove in for the touchdown. Oklahoma had too little time left to score again. Nebraska won, 35–31.

On New Year's Day the Cornhuskers faced their other challenger, the University of Alabama, in the Orange Bowl. This time there was little suspense. Nebraska won, 38–6. After that victory, no one doubted that the Cornhuskers deserved to be national champs. In fact, some said they were the strongest college team in history.

The University of Nebraska is in Lincoln, the Nebraska state capital. Memorial Stadium in Lincoln seats 76,000 fans. The school colors are scarlet and cream.

Nebraska's top man, Coach Bob Devaney, gets a free ride after the Cornhuskers' big gridiron victory.

New England Patriots

The cold wind swept across the Buffalo field in gusty swirls. As it whipped into Babe Parilli's face, the Patriot quarterback stared at his stumpy field-goal kicker, Gino Cappelletti. Both men were very concerned about the wind.

The Patriots were lining up to try to kick a 28-yard field goal. This was no ordinary game. It was the 1963 playoff for the Eastern Division championship of the American Football League.

The Buffalo Bill linemen crouched to block the kick. Babe knelt a few yards behind the center and took the snap. As he placed down the ball, Gino stepped forward and kicked. The ball arched high into the blustery wind, quivered, then dropped—right between the goal posts. The Patriots led, 3–0.

They went on to beat the Bills, 26–8. Then they flew west to meet the San Diego Chargers for the championship of the AFL. The Chargers demolished the Patriots, 51–10, and more than a dozen years passed before the Patriots got into another playoff for a championship.

The Boston Patriots were one of the eight teams that formed the new AFL in 1960. Their great players in the sixties were Gino Cappelletti, a pass catcher and kicker who became the AFL's all-time highest scorer; fullback Jim Nance, who led the league in rushing two years in a row; and strong-armed quarterback Vito (Babe) Parilli. On defense their best players were tackle Houston Antwine and fast-stepping linebacker Nick

The Louisiana Superdome, home of the New Orleans Saints, is part of a sports and convention complex that covers 52 acres of land. One of its innovative features is a six-sided superscreen television that can be lowered by cable from the ceiling of the stadium to allow fans in the stands to see a play as it is being shown on television or in instant replay.

Buoniconti, later a star for Miami. But only once—in 1963—did the Patriots rise to the AFL championship game.

In 1970 the Patriots came into the NFL with the other AFL teams. In 1971 they moved to their new stadium in Foxboro, Massachusetts, and became the New England Patriots. Their new quarterback, Jim Plunkett, tossed a lot of touchdown passes, but the Patriots stumbled too often on running plays and on defense. In 1976 the young, fiery Steve Grogan replaced Plunkett as quarterback. With a smoother attack and tighter defense, the Patriots finished second in the AFL East and became one of the eight teams to enter the playoffs. The Patriots were beaten in the playoffs by the Oakland Raiders, but as Grogan said during the season, "Nobody laughs at the Patriots anymore."

The Patriots' colors are red, blue, and white. They play in Schaefer Stadium, at Foxboro, which holds 61,279 fans. It sits on flat countryside 40 miles from Boston.

New Orleans Saints

Quarterback Bobby Douglass clapped his hands, and the New Orleans Saints broke out of the huddle. They trotted to the line of scrimmage—the 31-yard line, where the Detroit Lions crouched. The Lions were ahead, 6–3. So far their defense had been a stone wall against the Saint rushers. But Douglass had thought of a way to get around them.

He took the snap and faked giving the ball to fullback Chuck Muncie. Then he stepped back. As a Lion defender rushed forward to stop Muncie, a New Orleans pass catcher, Larry Burton, burst past the onrushing Lion. When Burton was four steps ahead of the Lion, Douglass arched a pass. Burton caught the ball on his fingertips and ran all the way to the end zone. The 69-yard play put the Saints ahead, 9–6. They held on to win the game, 17–16.

That nip-and-tuck 1976 victory gave the Saints high hopes for their future. They had joined the NFL in 1967, and in each of their first ten seasons they lost more games than they won. But the team has had some outstanding passers and receivers, most recently Archie Manning and Al Maxson.

The Saints play in the roofed Louisiana Superdome, the NFL's second indoor stadium. (Houston's Astrodome was the first.) The Superdome holds 72,000. The team's colors are old gold, black, and white.

New York Giants

Frank Gifford crouched at the line of scrimmage, ready to scamper toward the goal line on a pass pattern. His teammate, Giant quarterback Y. A. Tittle, rasped out the signals:

"Hut . . . hut . . ." On the second "hut," Gifford shot toward the goal line 14 yards away. A Chicago Bear defender clung at his elbow. Gifford veered, shook off the defender, then turned. He saw the ball flying toward him. Grabbing the pass, he sped into the end zone.

That touchdown put the Giants ahead, 7–0, in the first period of the 1963 NFL championship game. This was the third straight year that Frank Gifford and the Giants had battled into the NFL championship game. In both of the previous years, they had trudged away from the championship game as losers. But they were determined that 1963 would be different.

"We'll win this one," Gifford told friends before the game against the Bears at Chicago's Wrigley Field.

A little later in the game Y. A. Tittle lined another pass toward Gifford. This one was intercepted, and the Bears quickly scored to tie the game. In the third period the Bears plucked down another Tittle pass. Again the Bears plunged over for a touchdown, winning the game, 14–10. Once more the Giants had come close to the big prize and failed to clutch it.

Yet the 1963 Giant team, led by Frank

Gifford, was one of the all-time great NFL teams. During the eight years from 1956 to 1963, the Giants played in six championship games as the best of the NFL's East. But only once did they win the NFL championship.

The Giants were born in 1925 when a rich young sportsman, Tim Mara, paid a $500 entry fee to join the NFL. His Giants were New York's first NFL team. Mara signed two stalwart tackles, Steve Owens (later the Giant coach) and Cal Hubbard. The Giants won the NFL pennant in 1927 with an 11–1–1 record.

Mara continued to strengthen the team. He added a bulldog center, Mel Hein, and halfback Ken Strong. In those days players were on the field 60 minutes, playing both

Wearing sneakers, the Giants' Ed Danowski (22) makes a short gain during the famous 1934 "sneaker" game against the Bears.

offense and defense. Ken Strong was a triple-threat on offense. He could pass the ball, run with it, or kick it. And on defense, he and Hein chopped down their opponents' ball carriers.

In 1933 the Giants met the Bears in the first NFL championship game. The Bears' Bronko Nagurski thundered toward the Giant line, then suddenly stopped and arched a pass over the Giants. That pass gave the Bears a touchdown—a touchdown that beat the Giants, 23–21.

A year later the Giants were the Eastern champs again. And once more they met the same Western champions, the Bears. This time the two teams played in New York's old Polo Grounds on a freezing-cold day. The field was as hard and slippery as an icy street. Players skidded in their cleats, falling down as they tried to dodge and tackle. But the

Giant star Y. A. Tittle lines out a pass in the 1963 NFL championship game against the Chicago Bears.

Bears' bull-like Nagurski could not be stopped. At the half the Bears led, 10–3.

During half time the Giants put on sneakers that had been rushed by messenger to the Polo Grounds from a nearby college. As a result, the Giants' sure-footed runners flashed past the slipping Bears in the second half. The Giants scored 27 points in the final quarter to win, 30–13.

In 1938 the Giants won their third NFL championship. With players such as Tuffy Leemans and Ward Cuff, they beat Green Bay, 23–17.

The Giants won their fourth championship game by once again wearing sneakers on an icy field. This happened in 1956, and once again they were pitted against the Bears. The Giant team had a fearsome defense that included end Andy Robustelli, linebacker Sam Huff, and pass interceptor Emlen Tunnell. They also had a lightning offense with passer Charlie Conerly and pass receivers Frank Gifford and Kyle Rote. The Giants came onto the icy Yankee Stadium field in sneakers and shot by the slipping Bears, 47–7.

Then came disappointments. In 1958 they lost the NFL title game to the Colts, 23–17, in sudden-death overtime. In 1959 the Colts beat them again, 31–16. In 1961 they lost to the Packers, 37–0. And the next year the Packers repeated their victory, this time by a score of 16–7. Then in 1963 there was that heartbreaking 14–10 loss to the Bears.

Gifford retired and became a television announcer. Other stars retired. The Giants slipped in the standings. Since 1970 they have played in the NFC's East. Most seasons the team has lagged in the lower depths, though their fans have continued to dream of the days when the Giants really were giants.

The team now plays in 76,000-seat Giants Stadium at East Rutherford, New Jersey. Team colors are blue, red, and white.

New York Jets

Hundreds of fans were sitting at tables in a Miami restaurant, waiting for Joe Namath to make a speech. In just three days Namath and the Jets would meet the Baltimore Colts in the 1969 Super Bowl.

"Most people don't give us a chance," Namath told the fans. Many of the people in the audience smiled, for they knew the experts were predicting that the Colts would demolish the Jets by 18 or more points.

"But I think we have a chance," Namath continued. "Matter of fact, I think we'll win it. . . . I guarantee it."

The next day millions of fans were laughing at the boldness of Namath. His Jets were good, people said, but they would be crushed under the Colt steamroller. This would be the third Super Bowl. In the first two, the champions of the National Football League had demolished the champions of the young American Football League. The powerful Colts of the NFL seemed sure to repeat the performance against Namath's Jets.

Jet coach Weeb Ewbank decided on a simple strategy against Baltimore: quick rushes at the middle by running backs Emerson

Boozer and Matt Snell, plus short passes from Namath to flanker George Sauer.

The strategy worked. The Jets drove 80 yards for a touchdown, and led, 7–0. A little later the Colts fumbled near their own goal line. The Jets pounced on the ball. Then Jim Turner booted a field goal. The Jets led, 10–0. Some 75,000 fans, sitting in Miami's Orange Bowl, began to wonder: Are we seeing one of football's greatest upsets?

Indeed they were. The Jets, playing cautiously, moved close enough to the Colt goal line to kick two more three-pointers. They won, 16–7.

The Jets were called the Titans when they started as original members of the American Football League in 1960. The Titans played in New York's old Polo Grounds in front of empty seats. Often there were as few as 5,000 spectators at a game. Then millionaire Sonny Werblin bought the team and renamed it the Jets. In 1965 he signed Joe Namath to a three-year contract for $425,000, the most money paid up to then to any football player. The Jets began to win.

After the 1969 Super Bowl victory, however, their best players became older and slower. In 1970, when the NFL and AFL merged, the team moved into the Eastern Division of the NFL's American Football Conference (AFC). Not once during the Jets' first seven years in the NFL did the team enjoy a winning season.

The Jets play in New York's Shea Stadium. Capacity is 60,000. The team's colors are kelly green and white.

Notre Dame, University of

Other teams may have fans as devoted as Notre Dame's. But no school has so many. From coast to coast, in the city and in the countryside, millions root for the Fighting

Irish. The Notre Dame football tradition is long and distinguished.

That long tradition was put to a big test on the last day of 1973 when Notre Dame met the University of Alabama in the Sugar Bowl. Both teams had won all their games for the season, and it seemed certain that the winner of the Sugar Bowl would be named national champion.

Going into the fourth quarter, Notre Dame was ahead, 21–17. But then Alabama's Crimson Tide scored a touchdown. Although they missed the extra point, they were still ahead, 23–21. The Irish got the ball and drove all the way to the 9-yard line. On fourth down, Notre Dame kicker Bob Thomas kicked a perfect field goal to put Notre Dame ahead by one slim point.

The Irish defense held Alabama back in its own territory. And with only three minutes left, Alabama had to punt. The game seemed to be over. But a super kick, which rolled out of bounds on the Notre Dame 1-yard line, gave Alabama rooters new hope. A safety or an Irish fumble could win the game for the Crimson Tide.

Irish quarterback Tom Clements ran two plays that gained only seven yards. The third play was called back for a penalty. It was third down, eight yards to go for Notre Dame on its 3-yard line. Clements could not afford a mistake. Everyone expected him to run one more play, then use the Irish punter to get the team out of danger.

The ball was snapped and Clements seemed to hand off to the halfback. But it was a fake. Clements still had the ball and he was fading back into his end zone. If he was tackled there, Notre Dame would lose. Clements cocked his arm and threw a long pass to tight end Robin Weber, who made a spectacular catch on the 35. The daring of Tom Clements had put the Irish out of danger. They didn't score again, but they held on to the ball until the clock ran out. Notre Dame won, 24–23, and the team was named national champion.

This was only one of many dramatic victories for Notre Dame. The first came in 1913 when the team defeated Army by using a terrific passing attack. The main receiver on that team was Knute Rockne, who became head coach in 1918. In 13 seasons he won more than 100 games and became the most famous college coach the game has ever known. (*See* Rockne, Knute.) The Irish also boasted strong teams in later years, winning national championships in 1946, 1947, 1953, 1966, 1973, and 1977.

Notre Dame is a Roman Catholic university in South Bend, Indiana. The Irish athletic colors are gold and blue—not green, as many fans think. Notre Dame Stadium seats 59,000.

Notre Dame quarterback Tom Clements, whose pass saved the day for the Irish in their 1973 Sugar Bowl game against Alabama.

A jubilant John Madden cheers for his Oakland Raiders at the 1977 Super Bowl.

Oakland Raiders

"We can run at their right side and make big yardage," the Oakland coach, John Madden, said to his quarterback, Ken Stabler. The two men were seated in a small room watching a film. The movie showed the Minnesota Vikings' defensive line in action during a game played earlier in the season.

"Our linemen can open holes on their right side," Madden told Stabler, "because our guys are younger and faster." Stabler nodded. He and Madden were plotting strategy for the 1977 Super Bowl, the game that would match the Raiders against the Minnesota Vikings.

Two weeks later some 100,000 screaming fans sat in Pasadena's Rose Bowl as the Raiders lined up for the first running play of the game. Stabler, hunched over the center, called the signals. He gave the ball to an Oakland runner, who plowed into the right side of the Minnesota line. He was stopped after only a one-yard gain.

But Stabler and Madden stuck to their

strategy. Two big Oakland linemen, Art Shell and Gene Upshaw, hammered at the right side of the Viking line. The Minnesota right side began to give, then it cracked. Oakland runners dashed through gaping holes for long gains. The Raiders rolled for 266 yards, the most ever gained by one team in a Super Bowl. The Oakland players were easy 32–14 winners, as well as the proud owners of their first NFL championship.

The Raiders trace their history back to 1960. They were one of the eight teams that began the American Football League. From 1960 to 1966 the Raiders were nearly always one of the best teams in the AFL, but they usually finished behind Kansas City or San Diego in the Western Division. Like most AFL teams, they threw a lot of passes, mostly to receiver Art Powell and halfback Clem Daniels. In 1967 their coach, Al Davis, made a shrewd trade with Buffalo and obtained quarterback Daryle Lamonica. With Lamonica passing to ends Billy Cannon and young Fred Biletnikoff, the Raiders won 13

of 14 games. The 1967 AFL championship was theirs! They went on to the Super Bowl, where they met the high-powered Green Bay Packers. "We were scared out of our pants," Biletnikoff later said. The Packers shattered the Raiders, 33–14.

But the Raiders bounced back to win the AFL's Western Division titles in 1968 and 1969. (Their coach was now the burly, red-headed John Madden.) In both 1968 and 1969, however, the Raiders lost the game for the AFL championship.

Then in 1970 the two pro leagues merged, and the Raiders became part of the AFC's Western Division. Their quarterback was the left-handed Ken Stabler; their best running back, the rugged Pete Banaszak; their center, "Iron Man" Jim Otto. (Otto wore the numerals 00 and played in every Raider game from 1960 to 1974). Their best pass catcher was still the elusive Fred Biletnikoff. On defense the Raiders became famous as the hardest-hitting team in football.

In 1976 the Raiders won their fifth

Oakland Raider receiver Fred Biletnikoff catches a Stabler pass only to be downed by Minnesota's Bobby Bryant during the 1977 Super Bowl.

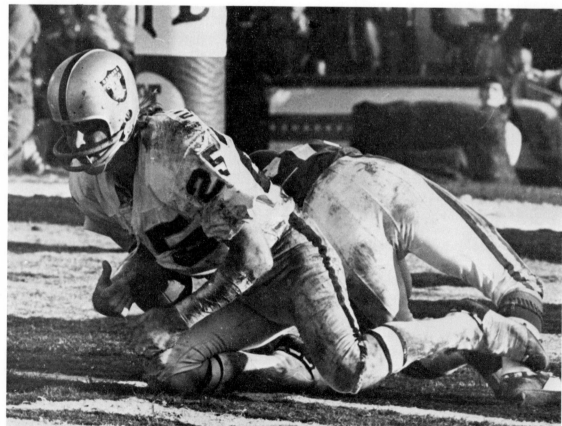

straight AFC Western title. Since 1972 the team had won 71 of 98 regular-season games, the best record achieved by any pro football team during those five years. But each year the Raiders were beaten in the playoffs. The "experts" were saying that the team always "choked" when it had to win the big game.

"They win all season," said fans, "but they can't win the big one, the Super Bowl."

At the end of the 1976 season the Raiders plunged into the playoffs again. They squeaked by New England, 24–21. They smashed the Steelers—winners of the two previous Super Bowls—by a score of 24 to 7. And then—at last!—they won The Big One. They overwhelmed the Vikings in the 1977 Super Bowl, 32–14.

The Raiders play in Oakland–Alameda County Coliseum, which seats 54,037. Team colors are silver and black.

offensive lineman

Football rules require that the offensive team have seven men on the line of scrimmage when the ball is snapped. Of these seven, five are considered offensive linemen all the time: the center; the two guards, who line up on either side of the center; and the two tackles, who line up outside the guards. The other two men who play on the line have different responsibilities. The tight end, who lines up next to one of the tackles, spends part of his time as a blocking lineman, and the other part as a pass receiver. The split end who lines up ten or more yards away from the other tackle, is primarily a receiver. (*See* diagram next page.)

The guards and the tackles do most of the heavy blocking for their team. On running plays through the line, they are responsible for opening a hole in the defense for the ball carrier to run through. This usually means that they must block a defensive lineman to the left or right. On running plays around end, one or more of the linemen (usually the guards) may pull out of the line and provide

The Vikings' Alan Page (88) charges Ken Stabler too late. The Oakland quarterback has already thrown a pass.

a blocking escort for the ball carrier. This is one of the more difficult assignments for many linemen since they must back up, turn, and move quickly to stay ahead of the man with the ball.

On passing plays, the linemen provide protection for the passer. Often, after blocking their men, they retreat slowly, helping to form a "pocket" for the passer to throw from.

Offensive linemen are chosen for their

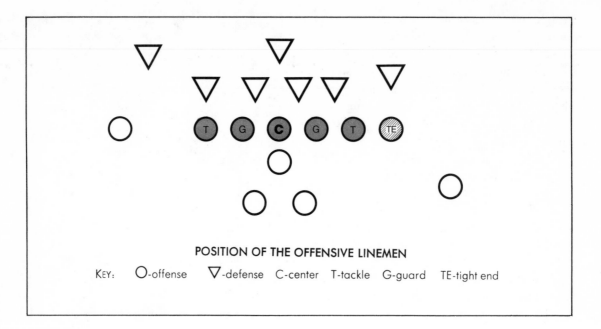

POSITION OF THE OFFENSIVE LINEMEN

KEY: O-offense   ▽-defense   C-center   T-tackle   G-guard   TE-tight end

size and strength. But they must also know how to block effectively. (*See* blocking.) And they must learn to carry out their assignments on every play. Linemen are not as spectacular as backfield stars. But they know that their contribution is at least as important.

offensive strategy

Of all the subjects football fans talk about, offensive strategy seems the most interesting. The spectators frequently claim to know what play a quarterback *should* have called. And when the home team loses a game, the town is always full of "Monday-morning quarterbacks."

How does a coach or quarterback decide what play to call in a given situation? There have been whole books written on the subject, but most football students agree on the basic approach. Football is a continuous battle of strength and nerve and wits between the offense and the defense. The aims of the two sides are exactly opposite. The offense wants to carry the ball downfield and score; the defense wants to stop the offense's prog-

ress. The offense wants to hold on to the ball; the defense wants to take it away. The offense wants to avoid costly mistakes such as fumbles and interceptions; the defense wants to cause them. And both want to fool and wear out the other.

Still, how would you know what play to call? To know the whole answer, you would have to know everything about a team and its opponent. But there are a few things that every play-caller must consider:

1. *Score.* Is his team ahead or behind? Is he protecting a lead or does he have to catch up with the opposition? A team that is ahead will not be as daring as a team that is behind.

2. *Time left and field position.* The team that is behind in the last few minutes must take more and more risks. The play-caller also changes his calls, depending on what part of the field he is in. Back near his own goal he must be cautious. Usually he will call running plays because it is too dangerous to risk a pass interception. If the team is near midfield, he can try a wider variety of plays. As he approaches the opponent's goal his job is both easier and more difficult.

On the one hand, he can use risky plays since it is unlikely that the other team will score even on a fumble or interception. On the other hand, the defense gets tougher when defending the goal, so the play-caller must think hard to find a play that will gain yards.

3. *Down and yards to go.* On first or second down a play-caller may be able to take chances—try a difficult play or even go for a quick touchdown. On third down he must concentrate on gaining enough yardage for a first down. If he fails, his team will have to punt or risk a fourth-down play. If there are only a few yards to gain, he may call a running play through the line. If he still has long yardage to gain, he may call a pass. His aim is to keep possession of the ball. If he loses that, he won't be able to score anyway.

These are only a few of the basic considerations. A good play-caller also keeps in mind what kind of weather and field conditions the game is being played in. He's not likely to call for long passes in a driving rain or for fancy running plays on an icy field. Then he must consider the strengths and weaknesses of his team and of his opponent, trying to pick plays that use his team's strengths against some weakness in the defense. If a certain play has been working, he may want to call it again and again. On other occasions, he may want to pull a surprise, calling the play the defense least expects.

Coaches and quarterbacks often work on a plan for a whole game. For example, they may want to try mostly running plays early in the game in order to test the defense and set it up for passing plays later. At some point, the play-caller will suddenly begin to call passes, hoping that the defense has been pulled in close to the line to stop running plays and will be caught unprepared for the passes. Most successful teams have a balanced attack. They are dangerous whether running or passing, thus making it more difficult for the defense to cover them.

Sometimes a player's personal strategy may play a big part in a team's success. For example, if an offensive tackle learns that his opponent, the defensive end, lacks good balance, he may practice special blocking techniques to keep the defender off balance. If this strategy succeeds, the blocker may give his quarterback an extra second or two to

THE FIRST CHEERLEADERS

Riding on a train to the field where they would play Rutgers, the Princeton players had an idea. If they yelled during the game, they might frighten a Rutgers player and cause him to drop the ball. The Princeton players practiced a piercing yell they called "the Scarer."

The time was 1869 and this was the first football game between two college teams. During the game the Princeton players shouted the Scarer according to plan. It startled the Rutgers players, but it didn't make them fumble. However, all that shouting must have tired the Princeton players, because they lost, 6–4.

Before the next game against Rutgers, some Princeton students decided they would yell the Scarer from the sideline. In that way, the Princeton players could save their strength for tackling. Princeton won, 8–0, so, from then on, all the shouting was done from the sideline by cheerleaders and fans.

complete his passes. That could make the difference between winning and losing the game. So football is not only a battle between teams. It can also be a battle between individuals.

offside

A rules violation called when any player crosses the line of scrimmage before the ball is snapped. *See* penalty.

Ohio State University

Most of the players on great college teams are seniors, players who have had three or four years of experience. But the 1968 team at Ohio State was made up mostly of sophomores. Of the 22 first-string players, 16 were untested. Their coach, Woody Hayes,

was one of the best in America, but not even Hayes could be expected to work miracles.

To everyone's surprise, the 1968 Buckeyes won every game they played. By the end of the season they were ranked first in the nation. As the Big Ten champion they were invited to the Rose Bowl to play the University of Southern California, ranked second best in the country. Southern Cal had an outstanding running back named O.J. Simpson. Fans thought that the Buckeye sophomores would wilt under pressure from the experienced Southern Cal squad.

The fans seemed to be right. Early in the game Southern Cal went ahead, 10–0. Then Ohio State quarterback Rex Kern began to throw passes. Woody Hayes was famous for his running attack. His teams usually aimed for "three yards and a cloud of dust" on every play. So Kern's passes were a big surprise. But they worked. By half time, Ohio State had tied the score.

In the second half, Kern was even better.

Ohio State quarterback Rex Kern calls signals during the 1969 Rose Bowl game.

Coach Woody Hayes

He threw two touchdown passes. The Buckeye defense held O.J. Simpson and his team to only one score. Ohio State won, 27–16. The sophomores had become national champs.

Woody Hayes was no stranger to championships. His 1954 team had been the best in the country. And Ohio State dominated the Big Ten in the early 1970s.

Hayes was a great coach, but his hot temper kept getting him into trouble. In 1977 he threw a punch at a photographer after his team lost the Rose Bowl game. Then at the Gator Bowl after the 1978 season, when his team lost in the last two minutes, Woody took out his anger on a player from Clemson University, grabbing him and trying to hit him in the face. The next day he was dismissed as Ohio State coach. His record of 238 wins against 72 defeats and 10 ties is fourth best in history.

Ohio State University is in Columbus, the state capital. The football team plays in Ohio Stadium, which seats 83,000 people. The school colors are scarlet and gray.

Oklahoma, University of

Football fans in the state of Oklahoma were used to winning. Their University of Oklahoma Sooners had been national champions in 1950, 1955, and 1956. These great teams under coach Bud Wilkinson had won the Big Eight conference title 12 times in a row (1948–59) and at one point they had racked up 47 consecutive victories.

But by 1975 the Oklahoma fans were getting impatient. Although the Sooner teams of the early seventies had been winners, they were not as strong as the teams at neighboring Nebraska. Then in 1973 Oklahoma was put on two-year probation for recruiting violations. As a result, though the 1974 team was the strongest in the nation, its games could not be televised and it could not go to a bowl game.

But the 1975 team was expected to bring football glory back to Oklahoma. Although fans grumbled when it lost a regular-season game and fell in the ratings, by the end of the season the Sooners were ranked second only to Ohio State. On New Year's Day, 1976, Oklahoma would play Michigan in the Orange Bowl and Ohio State would play UCLA in the Rose Bowl. A loss by Ohio State and a win by Oklahoma might still give the Sooners that national title.

On New Year's afternoon, the Oklahoma players watched the Rose Bowl on television. UCLA upset Ohio State, 23–10! So when the Sooners took the field against Michigan that night, they knew that a win would make them number one.

The Oklahoma defense played a heroic game, holding the powerful Michigan to one cheap touchdown. Meanwhile, the Oklahoma offense, led by quarterback Steve Davis, scored twice. Oklahoma won, 14–6. That week the team was named national champion. For the first time in 19 years, the fans of Oklahoma were completely satisfied.

The University of Oklahoma is located in Norman, 50 miles from Oklahoma City. Home football games are played in Owen Field, which seats 70,000 people. The school colors are crimson and cream.

Steve Davis hurls one of the passes that helped win the 1977 national championship for Oklahoma.

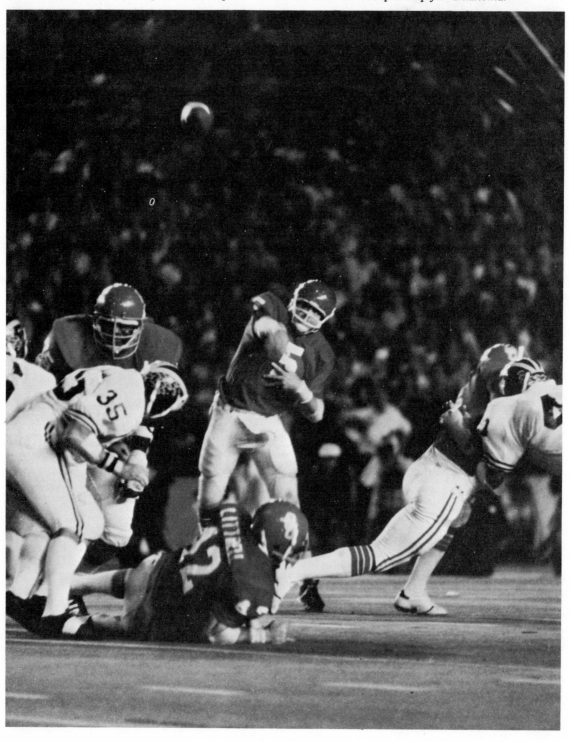

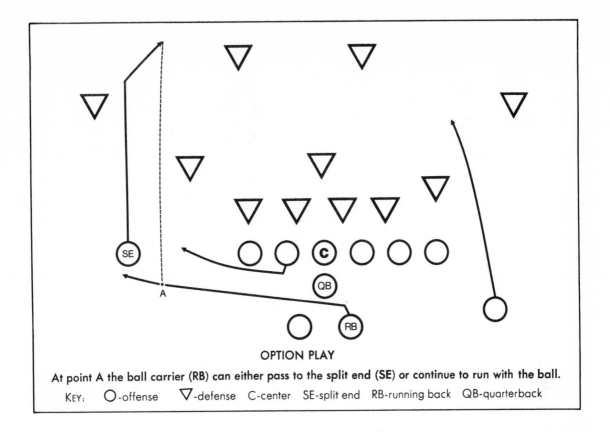

OPTION PLAY

At point A the ball carrier (RB) can either pass to the split end (SE) or continue to run with the ball.

KEY: ◯-offense ▽-defense C-center SE-split end RB-running back QB-quarterback

on-side kick

A kickoff technique used by a team that is behind and must try to gain possession of the ball in a hurry. The kicker lays the ball on its side, then kicks it along the ground toward the receiving team's front line. After the ball has rolled ten yards, it is a free ball and either team can recover it. Even if the receiving team reaches the ball first, it may not be able to hold on to it. On-side kicks bounce crazily and are hard to catch.

option play

A play in which a running back takes the ball, runs to one side of the field, then has the choice (option) of running with the ball or passing it to a receiver.

THE QUARTERBACK WHO WASN'T THERE

Quarterback Jug Girard rose groggily after being slammed down by a tackler. He wobbled into the huddle, called the play, then staggered toward the line.

Jug was the quarterback of a Green Bay Packer team during the 1950s. Jug got to the line and thought he was crouched over the center. Actually he stood, hands cupped, over the right guard—the lineman next to the center—who naturally didn't have the ball.

Orange Bowl game

The game played each year around New Year's Day between major college teams at the Orange Bowl stadium in Miami, Florida. The Orange Bowl began in 1935, and has become one of the four major post-season games along with the Rose, Sugar, and Cotton bowls.

The two teams that have appeared most frequently are Alabama and Oklahoma. Other Big Eight and Southeast Conference teams have also made regular appearances. The two conferences have agreed that following the 1977 season the Big Eight champion will meet the Southeast champion in the Orange Bowl.

Dropping back

passing

Every successful team needs a passing attack. For some teams, passing is the strongest part of their offensive game. For others, it is just a threat to keep the defense "loose" while the running game gains most of the yardage. Whatever its role, passing is important to every team's strategy.

The quarterback is almost always the passer. Most young passers concentrate on throwing the ball—learning to throw it hard and accurately. This is a big part of being a good passer, but the quarterback must also

work on other passing skills—dropping back, setting up, and finding his receivers. Anyone who can't perfect these skills will never get a chance to show how strong his arm is.

The quarterback receives the ball from the center with the fingers of his passing hand already on the laces. If a quick pass has been called, he may back-pedal only four or five steps, then set up to pass. More often, he will want to drop back five to seven yards. To do so, the right-handed passer turns to his right and runs back by crossing his left foot over his right. His upper body faces the right sideline, and his head is turned toward the line of scrimmage. He keeps the ball at chest level, ready to cock his arm as soon as he arrives in the passing pocket.

As he sets up, the passer looks for his receiver. When he finds him, he steps directly toward the place where the receiver will catch the ball and throws with a strong forward motion. The ball should be thrown overhand for best control. Many young pass-

Throwing

ers make the mistake of throwing off balance (without stepping toward the receiver) or of throwing sidearm to get extra power. Either mistake may cause them to lose control of the ball and throw a costly interception.

Probably the most difficult thing for a beginning passer is judging where to throw the ball. He must learn to make a split-second calculation, taking into account the speed and direction of the receiver and the speed of the pass. Only thorough knowledge of his receiver and hours of practice will teach a quarterback to throw "on target" every time.

passing records

See records.

pass route

The set pattern a pass receiver runs before catching the ball. (*See* receiver.)

penalty

Violations of the rules in football are punished by moving the ball five yards or more against the team that broke the rule.

There are three kinds of violations. The most serious are personal fouls that can injure other players. These include punching, tripping, blocking from behind (clipping), piling on, and roughing the passer or kicker. These violations call for a 15-yard penalty against the team whose player committed the foul. If a player continues to commit fouls, or argues with officials, the referee may penalize his team for unsportsmanlike conduct and even throw the player out of the game.

A second kind of violation is one that gives one team an unfair advantage. These include pass interference, holding, and illegal use of the hands. The penalty for interference is to place the ball down where the violation took place. The penalty for holding and other similar violations is 15 yards.

The third kind of violation is one that breaks a technical rule and usually stops play. These violations are generally the result of a mistake by one team. They include offside violations, illegal procedure, and the like. The penalty for these violations is five yards.

When a penalty is called against the offense, the defensive captain may accept or refuse the penalty. If he accepts it, the ball is moved back against the offensive team, but the down is played over again. If he refuses the penalty, the ball is not moved, but the offensive team loses a down. For example, the offense has third down and four yards to go and is called offside on the play. If the defensive captain accepts the penalty, it will be third down and nine yards to go. If he refuses the penalty, the offense will have fourth down with four yards to go. (*See* following spread.)

Time-out

First down

OFFICIAL
SIGNALS

Clipping

Personal foul

Interference

Incomplete forward pass

Illegal use of hands

Illegal motion

Offside

Score

Pennsylvania State University

Football was invented in the East. But in the 1920s the balance of football power shifted to other parts of the country. Although Cornell was the national champion in 1922, only two other eastern teams could claim the title during the next 50 years. They were Army (1946–48) and Syracuse (1959). But during the 1960s and 1970s one team came very close year after year. That team was Penn State.

In 1966 Joe Paterno became head coach at Penn State. At the end of his third season, Paterno's team was undefeated. It was invited to play in the Orange Bowl against Kansas, the champion of the Big Eight. If Penn State could win, its team might have a chance at being number one.

The game was a tense defensive battle, tied, 7–7, after three quarters. Then Kansas scored. With only a minute left in the game, Penn State got the ball on the 50-yard line. Quarterback Chuck Burkhart went for the touchdown on his first play, completing a spectacular pass to halfback Bob Campbell, who was tackled on the 3. Two plays failed to score, and time was running out. But on third down, Burkhart kept the ball and drove in to score as the gun went off. Penn State was still behind, 14–13.

Now everything depended on the try for the extra point. By college rules, Penn State could kick the ball over the crossbar and score one point or try to run or pass the ball over the goal and score two. Coach Paterno sent in the order to try for two. Burkhart threw to Campbell once again, but the pass

Penn State quarterback Chuck Burkhart in action at the Orange Bowl—this time against Missouri (1970).

was batted down. A jubilant Kansas team began to cheer as they ran toward their dressing room.

But a referee had blown his whistle. He had noticed that Kansas had 12 men on the field for the last play. Penn State would get another chance!

The players returned to the field. Chuck Burkhart took the snap and handed off to Campbell. Campbell ran the ball into the end zone, and Penn State won, 15–14.

But that dramatic victory wasn't enough. The football experts awarded the national championship to Ohio State, which was also undefeated. Paterno's men played undefeated seasons again in 1970 and 1978, but both times they lost bowl games and their chance for number-one ranking. They were the strongest team in the East, but they were still looking for their first national championship.

Penn State is in University Park, in the center of the state. Football is played in Beaver Stadium, which seats nearly 58,000 fans. The school colors are blue and white.

Philadelphia Eagles

The snow fell out of the iron-gray sky. It covered the field with a white, icy blanket as high as the players' ankles. The wind howled, blowing the flakes into the players' frozen faces.

The city of Philadelphia was buried by a blizzard. But 36,000 hardy Eagle fans had trudged over snowdrifts to watch the 1948 NFL championship game. They wanted to see if the Eagles, champions of the East, could beat the Chicago Cardinals, champions of the West, and win their first NFL championship.

For almost three periods the two teams had skidded and slipped on the icy field while the snowstorm whipped around them. Most of the time the players couldn't even see the goal posts through the thickening snowfall. Their hands were red and frozen.

The score was 0–0 late in the third period when the ball popped out of the numbed hands of a Cardinal. The Eagles' stocky lineman, Bucko Kilroy, pounced on the ball only 18 yards from the Cardinal goal. A few plays later the Eagles' fullback, Steve Van Buren, crunched over the snow from the 5-yard line to score the game's first touchdown. It was also the last touchdown. The Eagles won the championship, 7–0.

The Philadelphia team had joined the NFL in 1933, but for several years it was always low in the ratings. Then, during World War II, in the mid-1940s, Steve Van Buren came to them from Louisiana State. "Van Buren," an Eagle coach once said, "runs over people like Bronko Nagurski and runs around them like Red Grange." When tacklers hit his rock-hard body, they often got up with their heads spinning.

With Van Buren slashing through tacklers to lead the NFL in rushing, the Eagles led the NFL's East again in 1949. This time they faced the Los Angeles Rams for the championship. A pouring rain muddied the field. But Van Buren slogged through the mud to gain 196 yards, a title-game record. The Eagles won their second straight NFL championship, 14–0.

Slowed down by injuries, Van Buren faded during the next few years. So did the Eagles. But in the late 1950s they acquired a tough passer from the Rams—Norm Van Brocklin. "The Dutchman," as he was called, had been slowed by age. His arm often ached. But he could still sling passes like a marksman. The Eagles also had a hulking lineman, Chuck Bednarik, who was the last of the two-way players—a center on offense, a linebacker on defense.

In 1960 the Eagles once again finished first in the NFL East, playing the Green Bay Packers, champions of the West, for the NFL championship. Twice the Packers led. Twice Van Brocklin steered the Eagles into the end zone for touchdowns. On the last play of the game, Bednarik wrestled Green Bay ball carrier Jim Taylor to the ground only a few yards from the goal line. The Eagles were

In the midst of a raging blizzard Philadelphia's Steve Van Buren scores the touchdown that won the 1948 NFL championship for the Eagles.

17–13 winners of their third NFL championship.

During the rest of the 1960s and on into the 1970s the Eagles were usually back among the ranks of the also-rans. Today they play in the NFC's Eastern Division. Their home field is Philadelphia's Veterans Stadium, which has 66,052 seats. The Eagle colors are kelly green and white.

pitch-out

A lateral or backward pass from the quarterback to a running back. The quarterback turns from the line of scrimmage and pitches the ball underhand to the runner.

Pittsburgh Steelers

The Pittsburgh Steelers were leading the Minnesota Vikings, 9–6, late in the game. In

a box seat high above this 1975 Super Bowl struggle sat the owner of the Steelers. He was a gray-haired man with a long cigar clenched in his mouth. His name was Art Rooney. And as each minute ticked by, Art Rooney edged closer to seeing a dream come true.

Down on the field his Steelers marched toward the goal line. With the ball on the 4-yard line, Steeler quarterback Terry Bradshaw rolled to his right. He flicked a pass. It thudded into the arms of tight end Larry Brown, who tumbled into the end zone. Roy Gerela kicked the extra point. The Steelers led the Vikings, 16–6. A smiling Art Rooney puffed happily on his cigar. He was sure that his dream would come true.

A few minutes later it did. The game ended, making the Steelers 16–6 winners of Super Bowl IX. They were the 1974 world champions, a triumph that Art Rooney had dreamed of for more than 40 years.

In 1933, Art Rooney was one of the owners of a new team, the Pittsburgh Pirates, that had just joined the NFL. The team, which was quickly renamed the Steelers, had a few outstanding players over the years—halfback Byron 'Whizzer" White in the 1930s and quarterback Bobby Layne in the early 1960s. But nearly every season the Steelers lost more games than they won. By the late 1960s, to his chagrin, Art Rooney was famous as the only long-time NFL owner who had never won a championship.

In 1970 the Steelers became part of the Central Division of the AFC. That year they signed a college quarterback as their number one draft choice. Few fans had heard of him because he played at a small college. Blond and handsome, the quarterback was named Terry Bradshaw.

At first, Bradshaw played poorly—and the Steelers continued to be a losing team. But coach Chuck Noll quietly and calmly began to collect other quality players. From Penn State he obtained a 230-pound bulldozer of a running back—Franco Harris. Then he acquired a streaking pass catcher from UCLA—Lynn Swann. They joined older Steelers such as defensive bulwark Mean Joe Greene. By 1972 Chuck Noll had built a powerful offense and a defense so tight that it would become famous as the Steel Curtain.

In 1972 and 1973 the Steelers fought their way into the playoffs but were bumped out before they reached the Super Bowl. At the end of the 1974 season they finally made

Steeler quarterback Terry Bradshaw (12) hands off to Franco Harris (32) during the 1974 Super Bowl game.

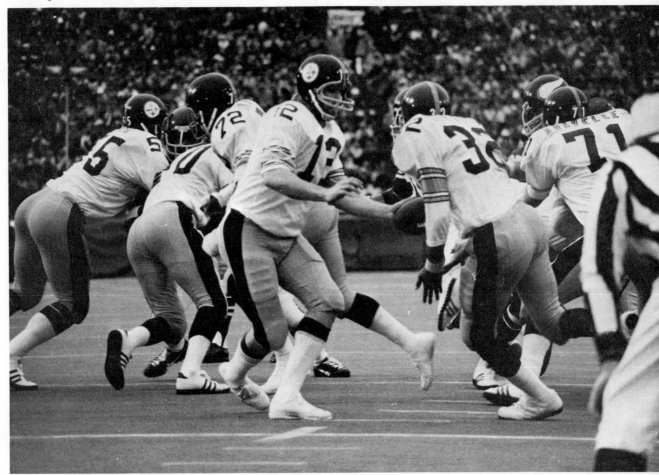

it to the Super Bowl, beating the Vikings. A year later they won the Super Bowl for the second time in a row, beating the Cowboys 21–17. In 1976 they went into the play-offs, hoping to be the first team to win three Super Bowls in a row. Their hopes were dashed when Oakland beat them in the play-offs. But in 1979 the Steelers became the first team to win three Super Bowls. In what was the most exciting Super Bowl up till then, they beat Dallas, 35–31.

The Steelers play in Three Rivers Stadium. Its capacity is 50,350. The team colors are the same as a pirate's colors: black and gold.

play-action pass

A play in which the quarterback fakes a hand-off to a running back, then drops back to the ball. The aim is to confuse the defense, not letting it know until the last moment whether the play will be a run or a pass. (*See also* drop-back pass; roll-out pass.)

pocket

The half-circle of blockers that forms about five yards behind the line of scrimmage to protect a passer. The passer drops back and the pocket forms around him.

prevent defense

A special defensive alignment that teams use when they must prevent a touchdown or a long gain late in the first half or near the end of the game. Prevent defenses usually have five men defending against passes and only three men on the line of scrimmage. The prevent defense may allow short gains, especially on running plays. But it is very difficult to throw a long pass for a touchdown against the prevent.

punt

A play in which the offensive team kicks the ball to the defensive team, usually on fourth down. The kick itself is also called a punt. (*See* kicking; the kicking game.)

quarterback

The quarterback is the director and most important player on the offensive team. In today's T-formation football, he lines up just behind the center, calls the signals, and takes a direct snap on every offensive play (except punts and place-kicks). The quarterback is also the best passer on the team. His throwing talent is very important, since some teams pass on more than half of their offensive plays.

The quarterback is also usually responsible for calling the plays. Even on teams where the coach sends in the plays, the quarterback may change the play at the line of scrimmage if he sees the defense is set up against the original play. (*See* audible.) In addition to his ability as a passer (*see* passing), the quarterback needs skill in three areas.

1. *Leadership*. Since he is the general of the offense, he must be a person in whom

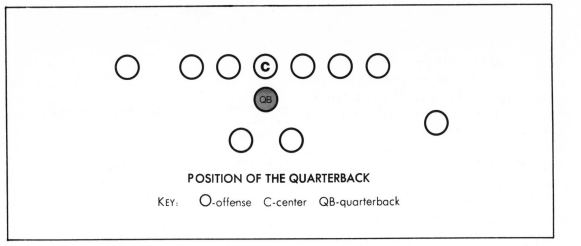

POSITION OF THE QUARTERBACK

KEY:　O-offense　C-center　QB-quarterback

the team has confidence. He must be able to take charge and yet give credit to others on the team. One coach has written that a confident quarterback can call a bad play and make it work anyway. But a hesitant quarterback will have trouble making the very best play work.

When he comes to the line of scrimmage, the quarterback checks to see that his men are set at the right positions, looks over the defense, then calls out the signals in a strong confident voice. If his teammates can't hear or understand the signals, they will not be able to charge quickly on the snap. Thus they lose an important advantage over the defense. A good quarterback earns the confidence of his team over a period of time. If he treats them fairly, never makes excuses for his own mistakes, and never blames others when things go wrong, the team will support him and help him perform at his best.

2. *Ball handling.* Even when he is not passing, the quarterback still handles the ball all the time. Coaches have been known to make quarterbacks carry the ball around with them all day and even sleep with it just to become familiar with its size, shape, and feel.

On running plays from the T formation, the quarterback usually turns after receiving the snap, and hands the ball off to a running back. It is the runner's responsibility to make a "pocket" for the ball with his arms. (*See* running back.) The quarterback's job is to put the ball into the pocket so that the back can grasp it securely and avoid a fumble. Young quarterbacks should make this kind of hand-off with both hands and should take care to follow the ball with their eyes until it's safe in the running back's arms. Proper timing for hand-offs takes hours of practice.

Quarterback's hand-off to the runner

Some plays call for the quarterback to make a pitch-out (or lateral pass) to one of his backs. He pitches the ball with both hands, underhand, taking care not to give the ball any end-over-end spin, which would make it almost impossible to catch cleanly. Pitch-outs must be practiced because if a lateral pass falls incomplete, the ball is alive and may be recovered by the defense. (An incomplete forward pass is dead and can't be recovered by the defense.)

One other ball-handling skill the quarterback must have is the ability to make convincing fakes. If he is faking a hand-off to a running back, he should put the ball in the back's "pocket" with the same motion he uses on a real hand-off. Then he has to pull the ball out and turn quickly, concealing the ball from the defense as he goes back to pass or hand off to a second running back. If he is to hand off the ball, then fake a pass, he should drop back exactly as he would for a real pass. His aim is to draw one or two defensive men, so the fake is useless unless it fools the opposition.

3. *Football intelligence.* A player who is "smart about the game" is better than a dumb one in any position. But it's particularly important for a quarterback to have good football sense. He should be watching the whole defense, noticing how it reacts to different plays and trying to find tell-tale signs of what it will do next. When he comes up to the line, he should be able to understand the defensive alignment at a glance and change the play with an audible if necessary.

Calling the plays, barking out signals at the line of scrimmage, handling the ball on every play, and carrying out the team's passing attack—these difficult responsibilities make the position of quarterback the most demanding position in football.

quick kick

A surprise punt on a first, second, or third down. Since no one from the defensive team is back to catch the kick, it may roll deep into the defense's territory. The quick kick is not often used in modern football.

receiver

In modern football, passing is often the most important offensive weapon, and a good pass receiver is an important player. He is likely to be taller and faster than most of his teammates. But his most important tool is what scouts call "good hands"—the ability to catch and hold on to the football.

A team may have as many as five receivers eligible to catch a pass. But there are usually two or three men whose *main* job is pass catching. One is an end who lines up by himself ten yards or more from the rest of the line. He is called the split end. The second main receiver is a back who lines up ten or more yards to the side of the rest of the backfield. He is the flanker. The third receiver is the tight end, who lines up next to the tackle on the side opposite the split end. He is a blocker on many running plays, as well as a receiver. The two running backs may also catch passes on some plays.

The receiver's first job is to get downfield to his assigned spot to catch the pass. In organized football, the play called in the huddle will tell him what pass pattern to run. There are dozens of patterns, and many have several different names. Some of the more common are:

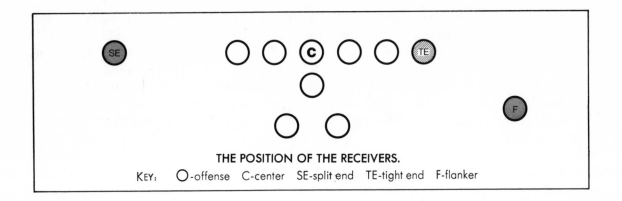

THE POSITION OF THE RECEIVERS.

KEY: O-offense C-center SE-split end TE-tight end F-flanker

1. The "fly," or "go." The receiver, usually the fastest one on the team, runs straight downfield, trying to lose pass defenders by outrunning them.

2. The "hook," or "buttonhook." The receiver runs at top speed to an assigned spot, then suddenly turns toward the passer to catch the ball.

3. The "post." The receiver runs ten yards straight out, then cuts toward the center of the field. His sudden change of direction leaves his defender behind.

4. The "sideline." The receiver runs straight out an assigned number of yards, then cuts on a right angle to the sideline.

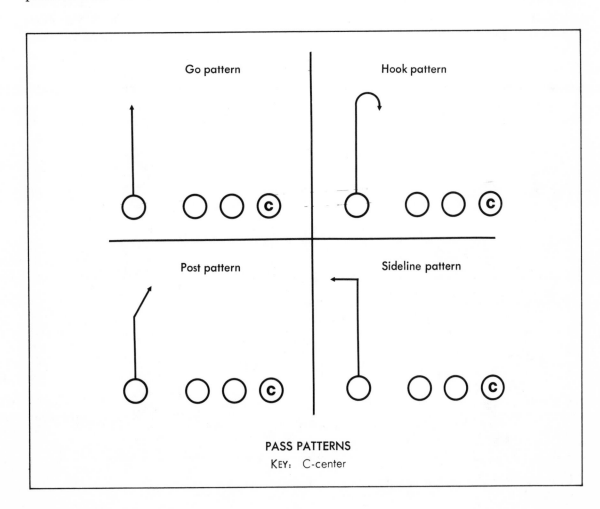

PASS PATTERNS

KEY: C-center

Losing the pass defenders can be a tricky matter, but the best receivers seem to know how to fool their opponents so that they are open to catch the ball. They use head and shoulder fakes, sudden changes of direction, and sudden changes of speed. They have one big advantage: they know where they're going and the defenders don't.

Getting loose and being at the assigned spot is half the job. The other half is catching the ball. Above everything else, this requires concentration. The receiver must keep his eyes and his mind on the ball and follow it until it is safely in his hands. The defender will try to break the receiver's concentration —one favorite trick is to shout "Look out!" just as the ball arrives. But the receiver must learn not to think about being hit by a jarring tackle or crossing the goal line until he has caught the ball.

Whenever possible, a receiver tries to catch the ball with both hands. If it is coming over his shoulder, he puts his hands out in front of him, palms up. If he has turned to receive it (as on a hook pattern), the position of his hands depends on the height of the ball. If it is coming at his waist or below, his hands will be down, thumbs out.

If it is higher than his waist, his hands will be up, thumbs in.

The most difficult skill for a receiver to master is timing. He is part of a two-man effort and must practice constantly with the passer so that the two of them develop confidence in each other. The most successful passing partners have worked together for so long that they seem almost to think together.

records

In football, records don't mean as much as they do in baseball. A good hitter in baseball will have a high batting average or a large number of home runs even if his team is the worst in the league. But in football, every player depends on the rest of his team. The greatest running back in the world will show poor statistics if he doesn't have good blockers to help him gain yards. A good passer will not be very successful unless he has good pass receivers to throw to and a good line to protect him while he throws.

Still, football fans enjoy talking about

A WINDY THREE-POINTER

Fans laughed when they saw Ross Caputo line up to try a 60-yard field goal. Ross kicked for a Salt Lake City, Utah, high-school team. His longest kick had been just 35 yards—and he had kicked only twice all season.

But there was a howling gale blowing at Ross's back during this 1970 game. So his coach had told him, "Don't punt. The wind will carry the ball into the end zone. Try a field goal. It will land short, but maybe it will stop inside the 10-yard line. Then they'll be in a hole."

The ball was snapped. Ross kicked. He toed the ball perfectly. It sailed . . . and sailed . . . and kept on sailing . . . right over the goal posts.

The 60-yard goal was the longest ever by a high-school kicker. And it was the only score of the game. Ross's team won, 3–0.

their favorite players' statistics, and there is always some excitement when a player is about to break a longstanding record. Below are some of the great records in professional football for kickers, passers, runners, pass receivers, and scorers.

	CAREER	SEASON	GAME
KICKING			
MOST POINTS-AFTER-TOUCHDOWN	**943**–George Blanda (Chicago Bears, Baltimore, Houston, Oakland, 1949-75)	**64**–George Blanda (Houston, 1961)	**9**–Pat Harder (Chicago Cardinals vs. N.Y. Giants, October 17, 1948) **9**–Bob Waterfield (Los Angeles vs. Baltimore, October 22, 1950)
MOST FIELD GOALS	**335**–George Blanda	**34**–Jim Turner (N.Y. Jets, 1968)	**7**–Jim Bakken (St. Louis vs. Pittsburgh, September 24, 1967)
HIGHEST AVERAGE YARDS PUNTING	(300 punts or more) **45.1**–Sammy Baugh (Washington, 1937-52)	**51.4**–Sammy Baugh (Washington, 1940)	
PASSING			
MOST PASSES COMPLETED	**3,686**– Fran Tarkenton (Minnesota and N.Y. Giants, 1961–78)	**288**–Sonny Jurgensen (Washington, 1967)	**37**– George Blanda (Houston vs. Buffalo, November 1, 1964)
HIGHEST COMPLETION PERCENTAGE	(1,500 or more attempts) **57.4**–Bart Starr (Green Bay, 1956-71)	**70.3**–Sammy Baugh (Washington, 1945)	**90.9**–Ken Anderson (Cincinnati vs. Pittsburgh, November 10, 1974)
MOST YARDS GAINED PASSING	**47,003**– Fran Tarkenton	**4,007**–Joe Namath (N.Y. Jets, 1967)	**554**– Norm Van Brocklin (Los Angeles vs. N.Y. Yanks, September 28, 1951)
MOST TOUCHDOWN PASSES	**343**–Fran Tarkenton	**36**–George Blanda (Houston, 1961) **36**–Y. A. Tittle (N.Y. Giants, 1963)	**7**–(Several players)
RUSHING			
MOST YARDS GAINED	**12,312**–Jim Brown (Cleveland, 1957-65)	**2,003**–O.J. Simpson (Buffalo, 1973)	**275**–Walter Payton (Chicago vs. Minnesota, November 20, 1977)
HIGHEST AVERAGE YARDS PER CARRY	**5.2**–Jim Brown	**9.9**–Beattie Feathers (Chicago Bears, 1934)	
MOST TOUCHDOWNS RUSHING	**106**–Jim Brown	**19**–Jim Taylor (Green Bay, 1962)	**6**–Ernie Nevers (Chicago Cardinals vs. Chicago Bears, November 28, 1929)

	CAREER	SEASON	GAME
PASS RECEIVING			
MOST RECEPTIONS	**635**—Charley Taylor (Washington, 1964-76)	**101**—Charlie Hennigan (Houston, 1964)	**18**—Tom Fears (Los Angeles vs. Green Bay, December 3, 1950)
MOST YARDS GAINED RECEIVING	**11,834**—Don Maynard (N.Y. Giants, N.Y Jets, St. Louis, 1958-73)	**1,746**— Charlie Hennigan (Houston, 1961)	**303**—Jim Benton (Cleveland Rams vs. Detroit, November 22, 1945)
MOST TOUCHDOWNS RECEIVING	**99**—Don Hutson (Green Bay, 1935-45)	**17**—Don Hutson (Green Bay, 1942) **17**—Elroy Hirsch (Los Angeles, 1951) **17**—Bill Groman (Houston, 1961)	**5**—Bob Shaw (Chicago Cardinals vs. Baltimore, October 2, 1950)
SCORING			
MOST POINTS	**2,002**—George Blanda (Chicago Bears, Baltimore, Houston, Oakland, 1949-75)	**176**—Paul Hornung (Green Bay, 1960)	**40**—Ernie Nevers (Chicago Cardinals vs. Chicago Bears, November 28, 1929)
MOST TOUCHDOWNS	**126**—Jim Brown (Cleveland, 1957-65)	**23**—O.J. Simpson (Buffalo, 1975)	**6**—Ernie Nevers (Chicago Cardinals vs. Chicago Bears, November 28, 1929) **6**—Dub Jones (Cleveland vs. Chicago Bears, November 25, 1951) **6**—Gayle Sayers (Chicago Bears vs. San Francisco, December 12, 1965)

reverse play

A play in which a ball carrier carries the ball in one direction (left or right) accompanied by blockers, then hands off to a teammate who is running in the other direction. (*See* diagram opposite page.) The aim of the play is to draw the defense to one side of the field, clearing the other side for the ball carrier. (*See also* end-around play.)

Rockne, Knute

The Notre Dame team was behind at half time, losing to a weaker team. The players, ashamed of their performance, waited for their coach, Knute Rockne (NOOT ROCK-nee) to come in and tell them what they were doing wrong. Maybe they could still win.

They waited 10 minutes, but the coach did not arrive. After 13 minutes had passed, the field manager knocked on the door and told the team they should be back on the field in 2 minutes. Where was Rockne?

Just as the players were getting ready to go back onto the field, the door opened suddenly and slammed hard. Knute Rockne had arrived, and he looked angry. He paced around the room glaring at every player. When he got back to the door, he scanned the room and said in his most sarcastic voice,

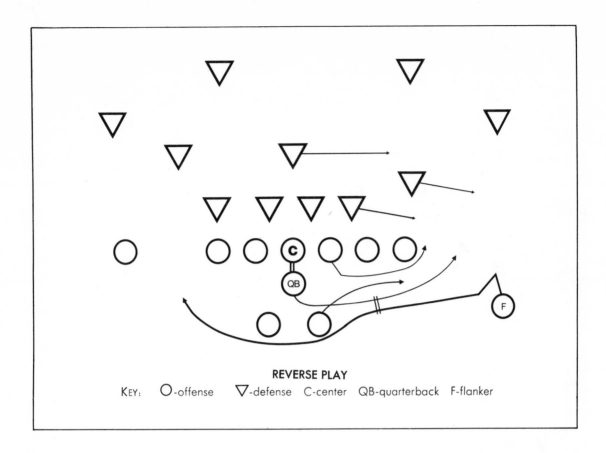

REVERSE PLAY

KEY: ◯-offense ▽-defense C-center QB-quarterback F-flanker

"Fighting Irish!" Shaking his head, he walked out and slammed the door.

That was probably the shortest pep talk Rockne ever made. But it fired up the players. In the second half they looked like a different team. They won the game by two touchdowns.

Knute Rockne was born in Norway in 1888. When he was 5 his family moved to Chicago, where he grew up. At the age of 21 he came to Notre Dame as a student and soon became a star on the football team. He was one of the earliest pass-catching ends. (*See* Notre Dame.) After graduation, he stayed at Notre Dame as a chemistry teacher and assistant football coach. Then in 1918, when he was 30, he became head coach.

During the next 13 years he became the most famous coach that football had ever seen. His teams won 105 games, lost only 12, and tied 5. They were not always bigger or stronger than their opponents, but Rockne

had taught them to play better football. And he always knew how to make them want to win more than the other team.

By 1930, Rockne's last season, the Notre Dame football team was the most famous in the game. The school in South Bend, Indiana, had fans in every part of the country. Many of its games were broadcast on the radio. Rockne himself spoke on the radio and wrote a regular column for the newspapers. His face and his voice were recognized by millions, and he was among the most admired men in America.

Then in March 1931, Rockne got on an airplane to fly to Los Angeles. The plane disappeared in a storm over Kansas. Soon the news flashed across the country. The plane had crashed, and all passengers had been killed. Rockne was dead. More than 100,000 people came to his funeral in South Bend. A few years later, his life story was made into a movie. He died when he was only 43. But nearly 50 years later, he was still remembered and admired as one of the great sports figures—and as college football's most famous coach.

Knute Rockne

roll-out pass

A play in which the quarterback runs to his right or left before throwing instead of dropping straight back from the line of scrimmage. (*See also* drop-back pass.)

Rose Bowl game

The game played on January 1 each year between major college teams at the Rose Bowl stadium in Pasadena, California. The Rose Bowl committee has agreements with the Pacific Eight Conference and the Big Ten Conference whereby the champion of each league is sent to the Bowl each year. In recent Rose Bowl games, the most frequent participants have been the University of Southern California and Ohio State.

The first Rose Bowl game was played in 1902. A famous Michigan team that had scored the equivalent of almost a point a minute during the season's games defeated Stanford, 49–0. No further Rose Bowl football games were played until 1916. Since then, there has been a game every New Year's. Between 1916 and 1947, teams from many parts of the country played in the Rose Bowl—usually against a West Coast team. Alabama, Georgia Tech, Pennsylvania State, and others participated at one time or another. Since the agreement with the Big Ten in 1947, only Big Ten and Pacific Eight teams have played in the Bowl.

For many years, the Rose Bowl was the only bowl game. None of the other games was begun until the 1930s.

roughing the kicker/passer

The kicker and passer receive special protection from the rules of football. The kicker may not be tackled when he is kicking the ball, or afterward. The charging defensive linemen may try to block the kick, but they must go after the ball, not the kicker. If they

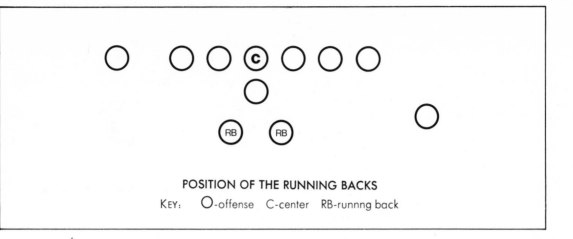

POSITION OF THE RUNNING BACKS

KEY: O-offense   C-center   RB-runnng back

run into the kicker, they will be penalized. (The kicker's team will probably keep possession of the ball because of the penalty.)

The passer may be tackled as long as he has the ball. But the moment he has thrown the ball, he may not be tackled or slammed down.

The aim of these rules is to prevent injuries. When one of these violations is called, it gives the offensive team 15 yards and an automatic first down.

running back

The job of the running back is to carry the ball and gain the yards that his team needs for first downs and touchdowns. It's important to remember that even the greatest runner depends on his blockers to make holes in the defense for him to run through. But great running backs are exciting because they seem able to create their own openings in the defense and to stay on their feet long after another runner would be on the ground.

The first job of a runner is to take the hand-off from his quarterback and protect the ball. A back who runs like the wind but can't hold on to the ball will never be a success. On most hand-offs the back runs by the quarterback. He makes a secure "pocket" for the ball with his arms and the quarter-

back puts the ball in the pocket. The pocket is made by putting the left arm across the middle of the chest and the right arm across the stomach. The area against the lower chest and between the arms is the pocket.

As soon as the quarterback puts the ball in place, the running back brings his arms together and grasps one end of the football with his right hand. He tucks the other end under his right arm and he is ready to run. His left arm is free to help him keep his bal-

The running back makes a pocket for the ball.

127

ance and to ward off tacklers. (If the play is being run to the left, the back may want to reverse the position of his arms when he makes the pocket so that the ball ends up on his left arm.)

There are two kinds of running backs. One is the power runner who is big and tough and likes to "run over" tacklers, breaking tackles as he goes. This kind of runner is often used in plays through the line. The other kind of running back is smaller. He relies on his quickness and deception to avoid tacklers. Both kinds of backs need some of the same skills. They both must learn to follow their blockers. And both must learn to keep their balance even when they are being pushed or pulled or when they are changing direction.

Running backs are often asked to fake— to run as if they have the ball. As they charge past the quarterback, he puts the ball in the pocket, then takes it out again. But the running back keeps running as hard as if he had the ball. If two or three tacklers are fooled into trying to bring him down, he has succeeded in keeping those tacklers from the real ball carrier.

Running backs must also learn to catch both lateral and forward passes. On some plays the quarterback will turn, and pitch the ball out to the runner with a scooping motion. The runner receives this kind of pass at about waist level. Both of his hands should be near his body, palms up. Like any pass receiver, he should concentrate on catching the ball and tucking it securely under his arm before he worries about where he is going to run. If he drops the ball on a lateral, the defense may recover it, so he must be careful.

Running backs also run pass patterns on some plays and should have the skills of a pass receiver. (*See* receiver.)

rushing records

See records.

safety (position)

A defensive back who plays farthest behind the line of scrimmage. His main job is to defend against long passes. (*See* defensive back.)

safety (scoring)

The only way a team on defense can score without getting the ball. If the defense can tackle an offensive player back in his end zone, the defensive team scores a safety worth two points. After a safety, the team scored *against* must kick off. (*See* scoring.)

St. Louis Cardinals

The Cowboys led the Cardinals, 19–7. Only five minutes remained to play. But the Cowboys knew they hadn't won this game—not yet. They were playing the 1976 St. Louis Cardinals. Pro football fans called these Cardinals "the Cardiac Kids." They had a reputation for stopping the hearts of their fans with last-minute drives to victory. "With us," said Cardinal quarterback Jim Hart, "nothing is impossible."

The Cardinals needed to go 68 yards for a touchdown. Even if they scored, they would need a second touchdown to win the game. Hart and his Cardiac Kids went right to work. The youthful-looking Hart flung pass after pass and the Cardinals swept to the Dallas 19-yard line. Then Hart threw a pass to Mel Gray in the end zone. The score became 19–14.

There were only 90 seconds left when the Cardinals got the ball once more. They needed to go 67 yards for a winning touchdown. Hart drilled the ball into the hands of his receivers, and the Cardinals swept to the Dallas 8-yard line. With only 13 seconds left, the 50,000 spectators in the Dallas stadium rose to their feet. They didn't know what wild thing might happen next.

Jim Hart dropped back to pass. He threw. The ball flashed right by the straining fingers of a Cardinal receiver as he cut across the end zone.

There was time for only one more play. Again Hart dashed back to pass. As he threw, there was complete silence in the stadium. The ball sped through the air and dropped—incomplete.

The score remained at 19–14, and the Cardiac Kids walked off the field as losers. That game was typical of Cardinal victories and defeats in recent years. Their games almost always seemed to be won or lost with hair-raising finishes.

The Cardinals were originally the Chicago Cardinals, one of the teams that in 1920 began what is now the NFL. The Cards were Chicago's first NFL team. (The Bears came to Chicago in 1922.) In 1925 the Cardinals topped the NFL with an 11–2–1 record to win their first NFL championship.

They didn't win another until 1947. That was the year they boasted the "Million Dollar Backfield." This quartet of famous All-Americas was lured away from the rival All-America Football Conference with salaries that were very high for that time—from $30,000 to $50,000 a year. The quarterback was Paul Christman; the running backs were Pat Harder, Charlie Trippi, and Elmer Angsman. They beat the Philadelphia Eagles, 28–21, for the 1947 NFL title. A year later they won 11 out of 12 games but lost the championship game to the Eagles in a blinding snowstorm that stopped the numbed Million Dollar Backfield in its tracks.

Through the 1950s, with the Million Dollar Backfield only a memory, the Chicago Cardinals always seemed to be at the bottom of the heap. One player bravely tried to keep them even with opponents. That was Ollie Matson, an outstanding running back of the day. He gained an average of 4.4 yards a try. But, more often than not, Ollie and the Cards were losers.

Desperate for good players after another losing season, the Cardinals traded Matson to Los Angeles in 1959, for nine—yes, nine—players. The nine new players didn't help. The Cardinals won only two games in 1959, and they were playing to empty seats. In 1960 the owners moved the team to St. Louis.

During the 1960s the Cardinals bounced back to warm the hearts of St. Louis fans with a lot of high-scoring games. There were big-yardage runners such as John David Crow and Johnny Roland, and touchdown-tossing passers such as Charley Johnson and Jim Hart. The passers threw to slippery re-

Cardinal quarterback Jim Hart

ceivers: Sonny Randle, Jackie Smith, and Mel Gray. Tall Jim Bakken strode into games to kick field goals that often gave the Cardinals a narrow victory. And on defense, safetyman Larry Wilson—the "wild man" of the team—brought fans to their feet as he blitzed through blockers to chase enemy quarterbacks. But though the Cardinals were nearly always contenders, they never went all the way to the NFL championship game.

In 1970 the St. Louis team joined the NFC's Eastern Division. They finished first in the division in 1974 and 1975, but both times they were eliminated in the playoffs.

The Cardinals play in Busch Memorial Stadium, which holds 51,392. Their colors are cardinal red, white, and black.

San Diego Chargers

"We've lost two out of the last three championship games," said the Charger coach.

"Let's not lose the championship a third time."

He was talking to the Chargers a few days before the 1964 AFL championship game. In 1960 the Chargers—then the Los Angeles Chargers—had opposed the Houston Oilers in the first AFL championship game. The Chargers lost, 24–16. In 1961 the team moved to San Diego. Again they were the champions of the AFL West. But again they lost to the champions of the East—the Houston Oilers—in the AFL title game, 10–3.

In the 1963 title game the Chargers faced the Boston Patriots. The San Diego team was led by veteran passer Tobin Rote, who snapped long passes to swift receivers Lance "Bambi" Alworth and Keith Lincoln. Lincoln was also a flashy runner; he weaved through defenses on long gallops for touchdowns.

"The Chargers are better than the Patriots," said the experts, "but they can't seem to win the big title games."

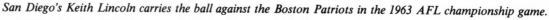

San Diego's Keith Lincoln carries the ball against the Boston Patriots in the 1963 AFL championship game.

In the 1963 title game, however, the Chargers finally came through. Keith Lincoln dashed 67 yards for a touchdown. Lance Alworth snared a long pass for another. The Chargers buried the Patriots, 51–10. It was the most lopsided score of any AFL championship game ever played. But that AFL championship was not only the Chargers' first; it was their last.

In 1964 and 1965 the Chargers were again the kings of the AFL West. They continued to win games with their new quarterback, John Hadl, who darted passes to Lance Alworth. (During an eight-year period Alworth caught at least one pass in 96 straight games, breaking Don Hutson's record.) But when the Chargers met the best team of the East, the Buffalo Bills, in the 1964 and 1965 AFL title games, the Bills' defense seemed to drop a blanket over Hadl and Alworth. The Bills beat the Chargers both times, 20–7 and 23–0.

After that the Chargers began to falter. In the last years of the AFL they finished behind Kansas City and Oakland in the West. Then in 1970 they and other AFL teams joined the NFL. During each of their first seven NFL seasons the Chargers, playing in the AFC's Western Division, lost more games than they won.

The Chargers play in San Diego Stadium, which holds 52,568. The team's colors are blue, gold, and white.

San Francisco 49ers

"We need a big touchdown play to get us rolling," 49er quarterback John Brodie muttered to his teammates. Hands on hips, he scanned the defense of the Washington Redskins. The Redskins were leading, 10–3, in the third period of a 1971 NFL playoff game.

Brodie decided to call a pass play. Moments later he gripped the ball and looked downfield to find a 49er who was open. He saw his lanky receiver, Gene Washington, sprinting away from a lone Redskin defender. Brodie arched a long pass. Washington caught it, then carried the ball into the end zone. The 78-yard play tied the game, 10–10. Just as Brodie had predicted, the sudden score sparked the 49ers' offense. They began to roll, scoring two more touchdowns and beating the Redskins, 24–20.

The following week the 49ers clashed with the Dallas Cowboys for the NFC championship, the final hurdle in the race for the Super Bowl. The Cowboys beat the 49ers, 14–3. So it was the Dallas team that went off to Super Bowl VI (where they conquered Miami), while the 49ers went home.

Over a period of 30 years, the 49ers thrilled the fans of two leagues with daring passers and streaking runners. Nearly every season the 49ers won more games than they lost. But every season they stumbled as they reached out to grasp a championship.

The team was founded in 1946. It was one of eight teams that formed the new All-America Football Conference. With left-handed Frankie Albert as the T-formation quarterback, the 49ers usually beat every AAFC team except one. The unbeatable team was Otto Graham's Cleveland Browns. They won the league championship in each of the AAFC's four seasons. In the AAFC's last game, the Browns topped the 49ers, 21–7, for the 1949 league title.

In 1950 the 49ers, the Browns, and the Baltimore Colts shifted to the NFL. Through the 1950s the 49ers awed both fans and their opponents. Their two big-yardage runners were Hugh "Nine Yards a Carry" McElhenny and Joe "the Jet" Perry, who were once described as "two bowling balls shot out of a howitzer." Their passers were the balding Y. A. Tittle and, later, John Brodie, both of whom shattered defenses with their line-drive passes. And at times the 49ers' defensive line resembled a bulldozer, especially when their 6-3, 270-pound tackle, Leo Nomellini, was bouncing back a ball carrier.

In the 1960s the 49ers' burly Ken Willard smashed through opposing lines while Brodie arched passes over them. But, too often, their opponents were punching through the

49ers' defense for touchdowns faster than the 49ers' offense was scoring them. The 49ers never finished higher than second in the NFL's Western Conference.

In 1970, after the AFL–NFL merger, the 49ers joined the NFC's Western Division. They won the division title three years in a row. But each year, in the playoffs, a rival team pushed the 49ers off the road to the Super Bowl.

The 49ers play in the 61,000-seat Candlestick Park. The team's official colors are 49ers scarlet and gold.

scoring

There are four different ways to score in American football:

1. If a team can run the ball across the goal line or complete a pass into the end zone, it scores a *touchdown,* worth six points.

2. If a team can kick the ball over the crossbar of the goal post on a play from scrimmage, it scores a *field goal,* worth three points.

Quarterback John Brodie calls signals for the 49ers.

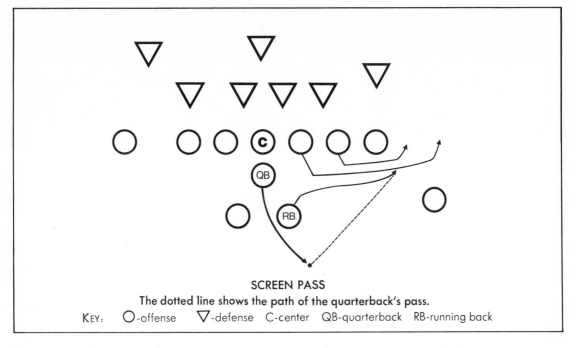

SCREEN PASS
The dotted line shows the path of the quarterback's pass.
KEY: ◯-offense ▽-defense C-center QB-quarterback RB-running back

3. After a touchdown, the scoring team gets a try-for-point. It may kick the ball over the crossbar from the 2-yard line or run or pass the ball over the goal. In professional football, either method scores one point, called the *point-after-touchdown* (PAT). In the college game, a successful kick counts for one point; a successful run or pass counts for two.

4. If a team's defense can tackle an opposing player in his end zone during a play from scrimmage, the defensive team scores a safety, worth two points.

After a touchdown and try-for-point and after a field goal, the scoring team kicks off. After a safety, the team scored *against* kicks off.

scoring records

See records.

screen pass

A play in which the quarterback throws a short pass to a running back who is protected by a "screen" of blocking linemen.

Seattle Seahawks

Pounding each other on the shoulders and shouting "All *ri-i-i-i*-ght, all *ri-i-i-i*-ght!" the Seattle Seahawks burst into their dressing room. There was a big grin on every one of their sweaty, dirty faces. For the Seahawks had just defeated the Atlanta Falcons, 30–13, in their very first triumph over a veteran NFL team.

The date was November 7, 1976. It was the first season for the Seattle Seahawks. They had entered the NFL with the Tampa Bay Buccaneers, whom they had defeated a few weeks earlier for their first victory. But now this new team had triumphed over the Falcons, a team that had been in the league for ten years. "This," said a proud coach, Jack Patera, "was our best effort yet."

The Seahawks' first players were mostly older men, but their first star was young quarterback Jim Zorn, who had been let go by the Dallas Cowboys. "They said I wasn't good enough," Jim reported after throwing a touchdown pass to beat the Falcons. "But I surprised people—just like we surprised Atlanta."

In 1976 the Seahawks were members of the NFC West. In 1977 they moved over to

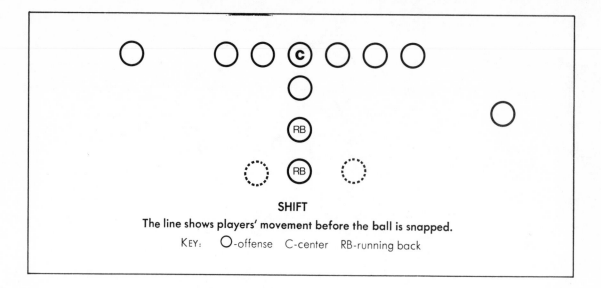

SHIFT
The line shows players' movement before the ball is snapped.
KEY: O-offense C-center RB-running back

the AFC West. They play in the new King-dome Stadium, which holds 65,000. The colors of the new Seahawk team resemble a rampaging sea: blue, green, and silver.

secondary

The defensive backs and linebackers, those who usually defend against passes and form a last line of defense on running plays. (*See* defensive back; linebacker.)

shift

A change in position by the men in the offensive backfield before the ball is snapped. The backfield may set, then shift to new positions. But each man must remain still in his new position for one second before the ball is snapped.

If the backfield is not shifting, one player on the offensive team may be in motion when the ball is snapped. (*See* man-in-motion.)

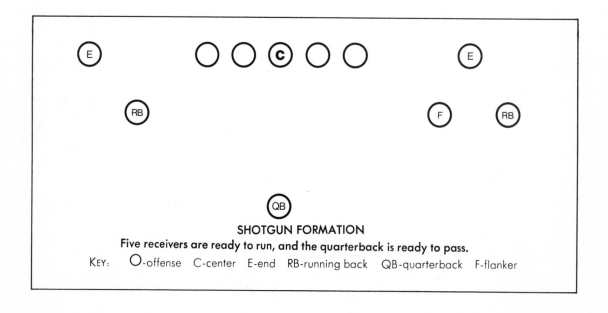

SHOTGUN FORMATION
Five receivers are ready to run, and the quarterback is ready to pass.
KEY: O-offense C-center E-end RB-running back QB-quarterback F-flanker

shotgun formation

A formation used by a few pro and college teams in passing situations. The quarterback lines up five or more yards behind the center, deep enough so he can throw the ball without dropping back. All five eligible receivers are on or near the line. At the snap, they can "scatter" (like pellets from a shotgun) on different pass routes. The shotgun is a weak formation for running plays, but excellent when a team has to pass and the defense knows a pass is coming.

Simpson, O.J.

The skinny 14-year-old boy was perched on a stool in the ice-cream parlor, seated next to a friend. Across the street they could see the crowd streaming out of the San Francisco stadium. The Cleveland Browns, led by their record-breaking fullback, Jim Brown, had just demolished the San Francisco 49ers.

"Look," the skinny boy said, "there's Jim Brown. And he's coming in here."

The smiling Brown ambled into the ice cream parlor with two friends. The boy strode over to Brown. "Mr. Brown," he said, "one day I'm going to break all your records." Jim Brown smiled and walked away from Orenthal James Simpson.

Some ten years later O.J. Simpson, running back for the Buffalo Bills, rammed through the line of the New York Jets for a gain of 7 yards. Then, having won the game, he walked off the field proudly while the crowd in the New York stadium cheered. O.J. had just become the first runner ever to gain more than 2,000 yards in a season. He had broken Jim Brown's one-season record by more than 140 yards. "I didn't just break Brown's record," O.J. said with a chuckle. "I splintered it."

Always cocky about his strength and speed, O.J. grew up as a gang leader on the streets of San Francisco. He was the fastest boy on his block whether playing basketball, baseball, or football—or running away from

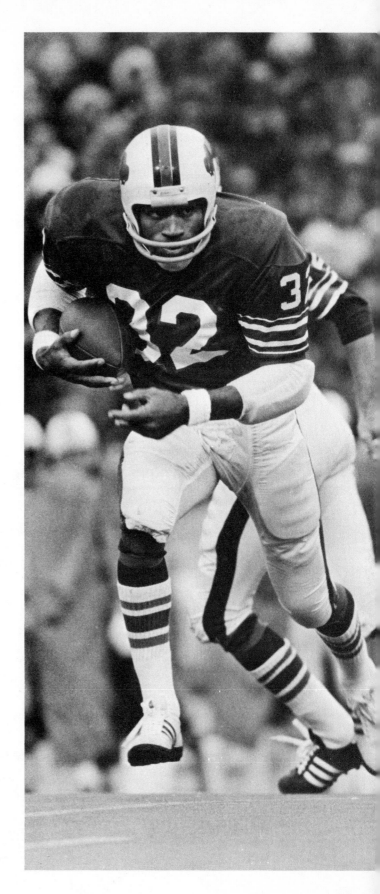

pursuing policemen. Then he got the chance to go to a junior college and, while there, decided to use his speed to be the successful man he had dreamed of being. After two years of dashing for touchdowns at the junior college, he went to the University of Southern California, where great runners Frank Gifford and Mike Garrett had thrilled fans with their twisting runs. In 1967 and 1968 "the Juice," as O.J. was now called, broke the records of both Gifford and Garrett. And each of those years the Trojans went to the Rose Bowl, winning once and losing once. During the Juice's two seasons, the Trojans won 18 of 21 games.

In 1969 he joined the Buffalo Bills. During his first eight NFL seasons the Juice led the league three times in rushing. In 1975 he ran for 23 touchdowns, more than Jim Brown or any other rusher before him had scored. But the Bills never had enough good players to enable O.J. to play in what he called "my dream game"—the Super Bowl.

In 1978 he was traded to San Francisco, his native city. Like Jim Brown, he became a movie actor. He is also a TV sportscaster and appears in commercials.

Southern California, University of

At the beginning of the 1972 season, no one gave Southern California's football team

Fullback Sam Cunningham goes over the top to make a touchdown for Southern Cal at the 1972 Rose Bowl.

much of a chance. The team was young and inexperienced.

Four months later, the Southern Cal Trojans were the only major team in the country to have won all their regular-season games. But they still had to face Ohio State in the Rose Bowl. Buckeye coach Woody Hayes—and many canny football fans—thought his team was the best in the country even though it had lost one game.

By halftime it began to look as if the two teams really were evenly matched. The score was tied, 7–7. The Southern Cal rooters were worried.

But the first time the Trojans got the ball in the second half, they marched downfield like a fresh team and scored. The second time they took possession they scored again. And the third and fourth and fifth times. Midway through the fourth quarter, the Ohio State defense was breathless.

Southern Cal's fullback Sam Cunningham had scored four times, and halfback Anthony Davis had gained more than 150 yards. The scoreboard showed USC 42, Ohio State 10. The poor Buckeyes scored once more later in the game. But afterward, Woody Hayes said quietly, "That was the best college team I've ever seen."

The Trojans had dominated the Pacific Eight Conference for years. Under coach John McKay, they won national championships in 1962, 1967, 1972, and 1974. And in 1978 they shared national championship honors with Alabama.

USC has produced many of the outstanding stars of college football history. From Frank Gifford in the 1950s to O.J. Simpson and Anthony Davis in recent years, this school was responsible for more great running backs than any other.

The University of Southern California is a private university with its campus in the heart of Los Angeles. Its school colors are cardinal and gold. Football games are played in nearby Los Angeles Memorial Coliseum, which it shares with the Los Angeles Rams and the UCLA Bruins.

split end

An end who lines up ten or more yards to the side of the nearest tackle. He is usually a pass receiver. (*See* receiver.)

Stabler, Ken

Ken Stabler's piercing eyes stared at the Viking line. The ball sat only a yard away from the goal line. "The Snake" knew what the Minnesota Vikings were expecting—a plunge by a running back.

More than 100,000 people watched as the teams lined up on the 1-yard line. They were there for Super Bowl XI, played on a sunny January day in 1977 in the saucer-shaped Rose Bowl at Pasadena, California. Ken "the Snake" Stabler and his Oakland Raiders led the Vikings, 3–0. The fans in the stadium were wondering: Would the Raiders—often called pro football's best team—finally win their first championship?

With a yard to go for a touchdown, the Snake faked a hand-off to a running back. As he stepped back to pass, he realized immediately that he had fooled the Vikings. They were rushing up to stop a run. Oakland's big tight end, Dave Casper, was all alone in the end zone. The Snake lofted a pass into Casper's hands. Now Oakland was leading, 9–0.

The Raiders went on to win the Super Bowl game, 32–14. In the dressing room quarterback Ken Stabler crowed happily, "We showed 'em. We proved we could win the big one!"

The Snake had also proved something else: that a left-hander could be a champion quarterback. Until Ken began accumulating touchdown passes, only Frankie Albert—a passer of the 1940s—had been a top left-handed NFL passer.

"When I was a kid growing up in Foley, Alabama," Ken once said, "I didn't even think about playing quarterback for our

sandlot team. I was a receiver. If a guy was left-handed, he automatically wasn't a quarterback."

Many coaches thought that lefties added a spin on the ball that made it slippery. But in high school Ken threw passes that landed cushion-soft in a receiver's hands. He also dodged tacklers on long runs for touchdowns. After one 80-yard weave through tacklers, a teammate said, "Ken runs like a snake." And Ken gained a nickname he never lost.

After his All-America years at Alabama, Ken joined the Raiders in 1968. At first injuries slowed him down, but by 1972 he was their number one quarterback. During the next five years he completed three out of every five passes. In 1974 and again in 1976 he led the NFL in touchdown passes. Each season the Raiders topped the AFC's Western Division, but each season another team knocked them out on their way to the Super Bowl—until that victory over the Vikings at the end of the 1976 season.

"That," said a Raider fan, "was the Year of the Snake."

Starr, Bart

Bart Starr bit his lip in anguish. He has just thrown a pass that had been intercepted. He trudged toward the bench, head down. There, hands on hips, stood the glowering Vince Lombardi, head coach of the Green Bay Packers.

"Starr!" Lombardi berated him. "You could see that the ball was going to be intercepted when you threw it. One more like that and you're gone."

Bart's face flushed with embarrassment. He slumped onto a bench. During this 1959 season he was the second-string quarterback

of the Packers. One more mistake and he would be dropped from the team. His dream of being a pro quarterback would go up in smoke.

Bryan Bartlett Starr had yearned to be a pro passer ever since his father, an air force sergeant, had taught him how to fling a pass. Twelve-year-old Bart had been the passer for a YMCA 100-pound team in Birmingham, Alabama, where he grew up. At the University of Alabama he was the team's number one passer—until his senior year. Then a new coach put Bart on the bench. Bart began to think he wasn't good enough to be a quarterback.

After he graduated from Alabama in 1956, Bart was offered a tryout by the Packers. Bart made the team, but only as the number two quarterback. The Packers were among the worst teams in pro football. In 1958 they won only one of 12 games. Then

Quarterback Bart Starr

Vince Lombardi became head coach. He told the Packers over and over that they had to get "mentally tough."

Starr began to understand what mental toughness meant—not giving up when you are losing. "If, when I throw a ball that's intercepted," he told his wife, Cherry, "I say to myself, 'What's the use?' I think that everything I throw is going to be intercepted. Instead I have to tell myself that the next pass I throw will be for a touchdown."

By the end of the 1959 season Bart, under the hammering of Lombardi, had the necessary mental toughness. He became the team's number one quarterback. Darting short passes and calling plays in a cool, calculating way, Bart guided the Packers to five NFL championships and two Super Bowl victories. (See Green Bay Packers.) He once set an NFL record by throwing 294 passes in a row without an interception. He completed 57.4% of his passes, the highest percentage of any passer ever.

Starr retired after the 1971 season. Later, he coached the Packers. The Hall of Fame ranks him fifth on the all-time list of passers.

Staubach, Roger

"Can you go deep on him?" quarterback Roger Staubach asked Drew Pearson, his wide receiver.

Standing in the huddle, Pearson looked at Roger and said, "Not yet."

"O.K.," Roger said, taking a deep breath.

Roger's team, the Dallas Cowboys, were losing, 14–10, to the Minnesota Vikings in the 1975 playoff game. There were only 50 seconds left to play. And the ball was 60 yards away from the goal.

Staubach hoped that Pearson, a swift runner, could shoot by the Vikings' Nate Wright to catch a long pass for a touchdown. But Pearson wanted to wait for the right moment.

Staubach called another play. The Cowboys gained a few yards. "Now can you go deep on him?" Staubach asked, as the Cowboys huddled.

"No," said Pearson." Wait one more play."

Staubach called another play. The ball was now at midfield, with only 30 seconds left. In the huddle Staubach looked at Pearson. "Are you ready to run by him?"

"Yes," Pearson answered coolly.

Staubach went back to pass. He flung a long, arching pass that Pearson, caught for the 50-yard touchdown that won the game, 17–14.

For years Roger "the Dodger" Staubach had tossed passes and dodged tacklers to win games in the last few seconds for the Cowboys. He had started his career as a high-school star in Cincinnati, where he was born February 5, 1942. Then he played for Navy, where he was an All-America in 1962 and 1963. Pro teams offered him huge salaries, but Roger had promised the navy six years of service in exchange for his education.

From 1964 to 1969 he was a naval officer, often on duty aboard rolling warships. Then he joined the Cowboys as a 27-year-old rookie. At first he and Craig Morton split the job of being the Dallas passer. But by the end of the 1971 season Roger was the number one quarterback. The Cowboys won the NFC title and then defeated Miami, 24–3, in the Super Bowl. Roger threw two touchdown passes and was picked as the game's most valuable player.

During the next five years Roger was nearly always among the NFL's top passers. In the 1975 playoff game, his last-minute pass to Drew Pearson nipped Minnesota and sent the Cowboys toward another Super Bowl. This time they lost to the Steelers, 21–17, despite two touchdown passes by Roger. After another great season in 1978 the Cowboys lost still another Super Bowl to the Steelers.

"We only lose," a Cowboy player once said, "when Roger runs out of time—and miracles."

Cowboy quarterback Roger Staubach looks for a receiver.

140

strategy

See defensive strategy; offensive strategy.

strong side

The side of an offensive formation on which there are more linemen (*see* unbalanced line) or more receivers. The tight end is nearly always on the strong side. Teams usually run more plays to the strong side of a formation than to the weak side.

sudden death

A name given to the overtime periods in pro football. An overtime period is played if the fourth quarter ends in a tie. The overtime ends as soon as one team scores. Losing in overtime is called sudden death because the game ends with the winning score, allowing no time for the loser to make a comeback.

Sugar Bowl game

The game played in New Orleans each year around New Year's Day between major college teams. For many years the Sugar Bowl game was played in Tulane Stadium. But beginning with the 1976 game, the Sugar Bowl moved to the new Louisiana Superdome, the world's largest enclosed stadium.

The Sugar Bowl began in 1935. Like the Orange Bowl, it usually features one team from the South and one from another region

of the country. The most frequent visitors to the Sugar Bowl have been Louisiana State, Mississippi, and Alabama.

Super Bowl

In 1960 a group of wealthy men organized the American Football League. Within a few years the AFL boasted that its players were as good as the players in the older National Football League. Fans wanted the best AFL team to face the best NFL team in a game for the championship of all of pro football.

Finally, in 1966, the AFL and the NFL agreed on a championship game—the AFL's best team pitted against the NFL's best team. The game would be played in January 1967, following the regular 1966 season. An AFL owner, Lamar Hunt, had heard his daughter call a bouncy rubber ball her "super ball." That suggested to Hunt a name for the AFL-NFL championship game— Super Bowl, a name it has kept ever since.

The NFL's champions, the Green Bay Packers, easily won the first Super Bowl, defeating the AFL's Kansas City Chiefs, 35–10. But the AFL got its revenge in Super Bowl III when its champion, the New York Jets, upset the NFL's Baltimore Colts, 16–7.

In 1970 the two leagues merged. NFL was kept as the name for the expanded league. Two conferences formed in the NFL—the American Football Conference and the National Football Conference. Each year the best NFC team meets the best AFC team in the Super Bowl.

The first Super Bowl was played in Memorial Coliseum, Los Angeles. Since then the game has been played in several famous football stadiums in warm-weather country —the Orange Bowl in Miami, Tulane Stadium in New Orleans, Rice Stadium in Houston, the Rose Bowl in Pasadena, California. Thousands of fans fill the stadium for each game, while millions more watch on television.

RESULTS OF THE SUPER BOWL:
1967—Green Bay 35, Kansas City 10
1968—Green Bay 33, Oakland 14
1969—N.Y. Jets 16, Baltimore 7
1970—Kansas City 23, Minnesota 7
1971—Baltimore 16, Dallas 13
1972—Dallas 24, Miami 3
1973—Miami 14, Washington 7
1974—Miami 24, Minnesota 7
1975—Pittsburgh 16, Minnesota 6
1976—Pittsburgh 21, Dallas 17
1977—Oakland 32, Minnesota 14
1978—Dallas 27, Denver 10
1979—Pittsburgh 35, Dallas 31

sweep

A play in which a running back carries the ball around an end escorted by other backs and one or more linemen who have pulled out of the line to block. (*See* diagram on opposite page.)

tackle

On the offensive team, a tackle is the lineman whose position is between a guard and an end. (*See* offensive lineman.) On the defensive team, the tackles are the inside two men on the four-man defensive line. (*See* defensive lineman.)

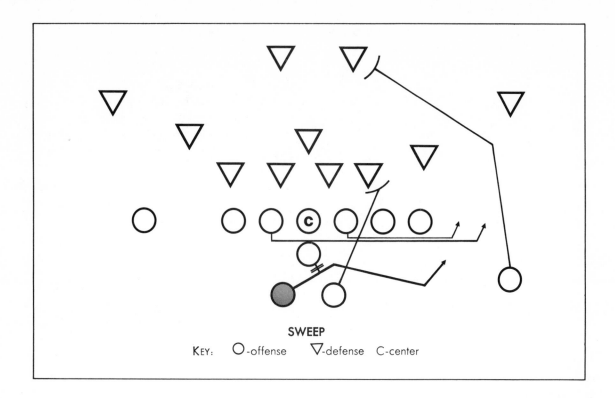

SWEEP

KEY: O-offense ▽-defense C-center

tackling

Tackling is the main skill in defensive football. Nearly every game is decided by who wins the battle—the tacklers on defense or the blockers on offense. Defensive players may sometimes gain attention by interceptions or by recovering fumbles. But their most important skill is tackling.

The players who tackle most often are the defensive linemen—the two tackles and two ends. Their assignment is usually to rush the man with the ball. But first they must get by the blockers, who stand between them and the ball.

Defensive players have one big advantage over the offense. They can use their hands, not only on tackles but also in getting past blockers. They can even grab the blocker by his uniform and throw him out of the way.

The defensive lineman usually takes a wide three-point or four-point stance. His feet are spread wider than the width of his shoulders, and his back is nearly parallel to the ground. In the four-point stance, both his hands are resting on the ground, fingers

spread, so that he can charge into the offense with full power. At the snap of the ball, the tackler charges the blocker, trying to get underneath him and drive him out of the play. Or the tackler may grab the blocker and throw him off balance. After making first contact with the blocker, the tackler

Four-point stance

143

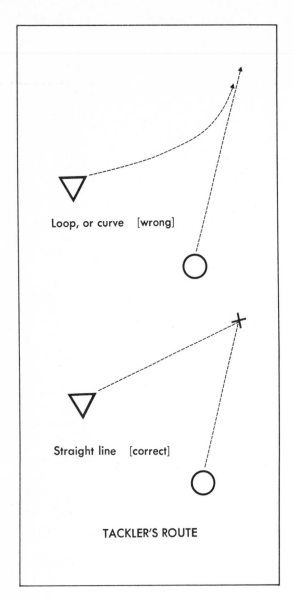

Loop, or curve   [wrong]

Straight line   [correct]

TACKLER'S ROUTE

tacklers. If the ball carrier is running in the open field, the tackler must decide instantly on the route that will allow him to cut off the runner before he gets away. The shortest distance to a ball carrier is always a straight line, *not* a loop or a curve. The tackler must consider his own speed, and the speed and direction of the ball carrier before deciding on his direction.

Making the tackle once he has reached the ball carrier is the defensive player's final and most important job. If the tackler makes a mistake, missing the runner or letting him get away, the offense may have a big gain or even a touchdown. The first rule of tackling is to use the whole body, driving a shoulder into the ball carrier, getting both arms around him and running him to the ground with the strength of the legs and back. In most cases a tackle should be aimed between the runner's knees and his waist. Lower tackles are too easy to shake off and higher ones often allow the runner to gain several extra yards, carrying the tackler on his back.

Of course, tacklers can't wait to act until they have a chance to make the perfect

The tackle should be aimed between the runner's knees and waist.

looks up, sees where the ball is, then gets there the fastest way. Other defensive men have more time to deal with a blocker and may be able to avoid him altogether.

There are a few simple rules for getting to the ball carrier after the blocker is disposed of. First, defensive players should keep themselves between the ball carrier and the goal they are defending. Very few tackles are made by men chasing the ball carrier from behind. Second, players who are approaching the ball carrier should try to force him toward the nearest sideline or toward other

144

tackle. If they can hit a man only at shoulder height, they should. If they can grab him only at the ankles, they should grab him there. Anything that delays a runner, or forces him out of his shortest path to the goal, will give time for other tacklers to come up and help knock the runner down. On an alert defensive team, most tackles are made by two or more men.

Tampa Bay Buccaneers

The Tampa Bay passer, Steve Spurrier, darted backward, ball clutched in his right hand. A wall of dark-shirted Cleveland Brown tacklers rushed at him. Spurrier glanced to his right. He flipped a short pass over a forest of arms. Tampa Bay's Essex Johnson grabbed the pass on the 10-yard line, then bolted behind his blockers into the end zone. Tampa Bay had tied the Browns, 7–7. For one of the few times in their brief history—this 1976 season was their first— the Buccaneers were not trailing in a game.

The Buccaneer team was made up mostly of older, slower players picked up from other teams. Seldom during their first season could they match their opposing teams. In this game against the Browns, for example, the Buccaneers stayed even for the first half, tied 7–7, but they fell behind in the second half and lost, 24–7. During the 1976 season, the Buccaneers lost all of their 14 games, usually by lopsided scores.

In 1976 the Buccaneers played in the Western Division of the American Football Conference. In 1977 they shifted to the National Football Conference. Their home field is Tampa Stadium, which seats 71,000. The team's colors are Florida orange and white with red trim.

Tarkenton, Fran

The purple-shirted Minnesota Vikings lined up opposite the burly Buffalo Bills. The Vi-

kings were leading, 28–7, in this 1975 NFL game.

Viking quarterback Fran Tarkenton glanced left and right as he called signals. The ball sat on the 6-yard line, but the crouching Bills were certain that Fran wouldn't call a running play. They expected him to pass—and for a very good reason.

Sure enough, Fran took the snap, stepped back, and looked into the end zone. He saw big Chuck Foreman swerve near the goal

Fran Tarkenton, holder of most of the pro passing records.

posts. Fran threw a sharp pass that Foreman caught for a touchdown.

Fran's teammates leaped all over him. He had just topped Johnny Unitas's record. He had thrown more touchdown passes in his career than anyone else—291.

By 1975 Francis Asbury Tarkenton had accumulated a lot of records. In fact, each time he *threw* a pass, he set a record. He had already tossed more passes—over 5,000—than anyone else. Each time he *completed* a pass, he also set a record. By the time he retired, he had completed more passes—over 3,000—than anyone else.

Fran had been a high-school passer in Athens, Georgia, and an All-America passer at the University of Georgia. He joined the new Viking team for their first regular-season game, and they beat the Bears, 37–13. Usually, though, the team lost. In 1967, Tarkenton was traded to the Giants, but he was traded back to the Vikings in 1972.

The team had been rebuilt by its new coach, Bud Grant. With Tarkenton needling short passes—"long passes are easier to intercept"—the Vikings won the Central Division title each season from 1973 to 1976. They won the NFC championship in three of those four years. (*See* Minnesota Vikings.) But all three times they were defeated by the AFC champions in the Super Bowl.

In 1979 Fran retired to become a TV announcer. He had thrown more passes (6,467) and completed more (3,686) for more touchdowns (343) than anyone ever. Most players agreed with his last coach, Bud Grant, who said of him: "Francis is the greatest quarterback ever to play the game."

Taylor, Charley

Charley Taylor trotted toward his position as wide receiver. As he stopped at the line of scrimmage, he glanced at the Eagle cornerback who was guarding him. Then he turned his head to watch his teammate, Redskin quarterback Joe Theisman, snap out the signals.

"Slow Motion" Taylor, a fast man on the field.

The Philadelphia Eagles were two touchdowns ahead of the Washington Redskins in this 1975 game. Victory meant little to either team. Neither had a chance to get into the playoffs and go to the Super Bowl. But this play was going to be very important to Charley Taylor—and to NFL history.

Theisman stepped back to pass. Charley, with his usual lightning speed, swerved toward the middle of the field. Then he angled sharply toward the sideline. The Eagle cornerback was chasing frantically at his heels. Charley saw the brown football spinning toward him, larger and larger. Charley stuck up two large hands and grabbed the ball. Then he was knocked down.

That catch was the 634th of Charley Taylor's NFL career. He had just passed Don Maynard's record (Don Maynard was a New York Jet) to become the leading pass catcher of all time.

Charley Taylor had come from little

Grand Prairie, Texas, to be an All-America ball carrier at Arizona State. In 1964 he joined the Redskins. The veterans dubbed him "Slow Motion" because he moved so slowly when he was off the field. But give him a football to carry, and he changed completely, slithering and slamming through tacklers. And he sped out of the backfield to snare passes. In 1966 he latched on to 72 passes, the most in the NFL that year, and he led the league again in 1967.

Charley stood 6-foot-3 and weighed just 200 pounds. The Redskins worried that his spindly legs might be damaged by tacklers if he kept on carrying the ball. They made him a wide receiver. Almost every season he caught more passes than any other Redskin.

"I've got a favorite pattern I like to run," he once said. "I like to cut toward the sideline a couple of times. The man who's guarding me sneaks closer so he can step in front of me and intercept the ball. When he's close, I shoot by him to catch the ball and there's nothing else in front of me but touchdown-land."

In 13 NFL seasons Charley galloped a total of more than five miles with passes he caught. A few pass receivers gained more yards. But none caught more passes than Charley Taylor.

Texas, University of

Texas had the ball, fourth down and three yards to go on its 43-yard line. The Longhorns were behind, 14–8, with only five minutes to go, so they would have to try for the first down. Quarterback James Street faded back to pass. He threw the ball far down the field, too far for receiver Randy Peschel—or so it seemed.

Texas player Jim Bertelsen (35) picks up yards against Arkansas in the 1969 championship game that sent Texas to the Cotton Bowl.

In the stands were politicians, movie stars —and Richard Nixon, the President of the United States. Texas was playing Arkansas for the Southwest Conference championship and the 1969 national championship as well. If Texas was to have a chance, Randy Peschel had to catch that ball.

He leaped high, got hold of it, and tumbled to the ground at the Arkansas 13-yard line. Two plays later the Longhorns scored, and the extra point put them ahead, 15–14.

But Arkansas still had time to score again. They drove from their 20 to the Texas 39. Then, with 1:38 left, the Arkansas quarterback fired the ball toward receiver John Rees. But Tom Campbell, a Texas defensive back, was in front of Rees. He intercepted the ball. Texas ran out the clock and won.

After the game, President Nixon presented the Texas team with a plaque signifying that the Longhorns were national champs. On New Year's Day they defended their title by beating Notre Dame, 21–17, in the Cotton Bowl. It was the second national title they had won in the 1960s, and they continued to be one of the great teams in the game, heroes in a football-happy state.

The University of Texas is in Austin, the state capital. Home games are played in the 80,000-seat Memorial Stadium. Team colors are orange and white.

Thorpe, Jim

The game was supposed to be a mismatch. On one side was Harvard, the previous year's national champion. On the other, the Carlisle Training School, a small trade school in Pennsylvania for American Indians. The year was 1911.

At the beginning, the Harvard team scored easily. Carlisle had trouble moving the ball near the Harvard goal. But the Indian school had a kicker who seemed to be able to score field goals from anywhere. During the first half he kicked them from the 23-, the 37-, and the 45-yard lines. And he was a tiger on defense, helping to keep the Harvard team from scoring. The Indians were ahead, 9–6, at the half.

Coming out for the second half, the Harvard players were fired up. They scored a touchdown, then a field goal. They went ahead, 15–9, and their fans relaxed.

But they hadn't seen the last of the Indian kicker. When Carlisle got the ball, the kicker decided it was time for him to run with it. And he did. He carried the ball on nine straight plays, and on the last he went over the goal for a touchdown. The Harvards stared with amazement at this young Indian who stood over six feet tall and weighed 190 pounds. Now he had tied the score at 15-all.

Harvard couldn't score again, but neither could Carlisle. Late in the game the Indians were stuck with fourth down at the Harvard 43-yard line. Thorpe decided to try a field goal from midfield. The ball flew straight and true between the uprights. Carlisle won, 18–15, in one of football's greatest upsets.

Who was the Indian who scored all the points? His name was Jim Thorpe. And football was not his only sport. The next year he won gold medals at the Olympics in the pentathlon and decathlon, the most demanding of all the events. After playing more football for Carlisle, he signed to play major-league baseball with the New York Giants. Then he returned to football to play for some of the earliest professional teams, including the Canton (Ohio) Bulldogs. He was even made the president of the new pro league that would become the NFL. In 1950 Thorpe was voted the greatest athlete of the past 50 years. Few who saw him doubt he was the greatest ever.

Thorpe's accomplishments on the playing field soon were legends. But the rest of his life was filled with difficulty and disappointment. He had been born in 1888 on an Indian reservation in Oklahoma. (His mother was a granddaughter of the great Chief Black Hawk.) Life on the reservation was hard, and Thorpe left when he was 15 to go to Carlisle.

A year after his great victory at the Olympics, officials discovered that he had played

Jim Thorpe, Canton Bulldog

cial list of medal winners. Jim fought for years to get the medals back, but he never succeeded.

He played football until he was past 40. By then he was fat and out of shape. But he could still play better than most of his teammates. After he retired, alcohol became a serious problem for him. He lived the rest of his life in obscurity. Once in a while he would appear at a newspaper office and talk to sportswriters about his days of glory. But he was a shadow of his old self. He died in poverty in 1953.

tight end .

An end who lines up close to the tackle on his side. A tight end is sometimes a pass receiver and sometimes a blocker. (*See* receiver; offensive lineman.)

try-for-point

The chance every team gets to score an extra point after it makes a touchdown. The ball is placed down on the 2-yard line, and the team may either kick it through the uprights of the goal post or run or pass it over the goal.

In professional football only one extra point may be scored, no matter whether the ball is kicked, run, or passed. In high-school and college football, the kick counts for one point if it is good. A successful run or pass over the goal counts for two points.

touchback

The situation in which a team receiving the ball must put it into play on its own 20-yard line. This occurs when:

1. A kickoff or punt rolls to a stop in the end zone, goes beyond it, or is caught and touched down by a receiver in the end zone.

semi-professional baseball before joining the Olympic team. They made him give back the medals, and they took his name off the offi-

149

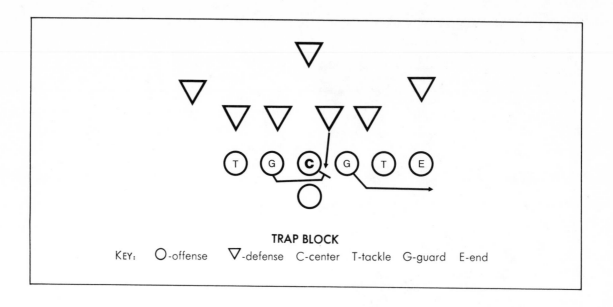

TRAP BLOCK

KEY: O-offense   ▽-defense   C-center   T-tackle   G-guard   E-end

2. An unsuccessful field goal lands in or beyond the end zone. A touchback is *not* a safety, and no points are scored.

touchdown

A score worth six points. A touchdown is scored when a team runs the ball over the opponent's goal or completes a pass into the end zone. (*See* scoring.)

trap

A blocking technique in which a defensive lineman is allowed by the offensive team to charge past the line of scrimmage. He is then blocked from the side by a lineman who has pulled out of the line. The defensive player has been "trapped," and driven away from the ball carrier and out of the play. (*See* diagram above.)

two-point play

In college football, a try-for-point after a touchdown in which the team attempts to run or pass the ball across the goal, scoring two points. (*See* scoring; try-for-point.)

unbalanced line

An offensive alignment in which more linemen are on one side of the center than the other. (*See* diagram on opposite page.)

Unitas, Johnny

"Why are you getting rid of this kid Unitas?" the reporter asked the Pittsburgh Steelers' head coach.

"Too dumb," the coach answered. "The kid was just too dumb to be a pro quarterback."

That evening, with ten dollars in his pocket, 21-year-old Johnny Unitas hitch-

E — T — **C** — G — G — T — E

← weak side → ← strong side →

UNBALANCED LINE

KEY: O-offense C-center E-end T-tackle G-guard

hiked from the Steeler training camp in upstate New York back to his home in Pittsburgh. There he tramped to work each morning with a bag of lunch under his arm. He had a job hammering in rivets on the girders of a rising skyscraper.

On Saturdays he *hut-hutted* signals as the quarterback for a sandlot team called the Bloomfield Rams. The Rams played before a few thousand people seated in rickety wooden bleachers. Johnny was paid six dollars a game.

All his life he had wanted to be a pro quarterback. As a skinny 145-pound teenager, he had been one of the best high-school passers in Pittsburgh. Big colleges—Notre Dame and others—rejected Johnny because he was too skinny. Finally he was accepted at a smaller college, the University of Louisville. There he set a string of passing records.

Veteran Johnny Unitas calls signals for the Colts.

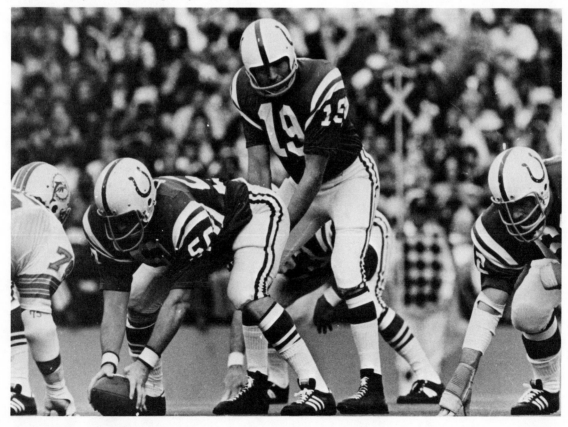

When he graduated he was signed by the Steelers, who gave him a brief tryout in the fall of 1955. They let him go. The Steeler coach thought that a player as quiet as Johnny was not sharp enough to call plays for a pro team.

So Johnny played for the Bloomfield Rams and hoped a pro team would call him again. A call did come—this time from the Baltimore Colts. They offered Johnny a tryout the following spring (1956). The Colt coach, Weeb Ewbank, stared wide-eyed when he saw Johnny's passes shoot with bull's-eye accuracy into the hands of receivers. At the start of the 1956 season Johnny was the Colt's number two quarterback.

Soon he became number one. In the 1958 game for the world championship of pro football, Unitas steered the Colts on a tense, last-minute drive that tied the Giants, 17–17. Then, in pro football's first sudden-death overtime, he shrewdly called the plays that marched the Colts 80 yards for the touchdown that won what has been called "football's greatest game." (*See* Baltimore Colts.)

Johnny U., as fans called him, went on to pitch passes that won two other world championships for the Colts. When he retired after the 1973 season, he had thrown more passes (5,186)—and completed more (2,830)—than any passer before him. He is ranked sixth on the Hall of Fame's list of all-time great passers.

And no one since that Pittsburgh head coach has ever called Johnny U. dumb.

University of California at Los Angeles (UCLA)

When UCLA went to the Rose Bowl in 1976, the team had real cause to celebrate. It had not played there for ten long years. Its crosstown rival, Southern California, had won the Pacific Eight championship during most of those years, and had gone on to the Bowl each time.

Unfortunately, however, UCLA was facing Ohio State at the Bowl. They had already played together once that season. And in the earlier game Ohio State had thrashed the Bruins, 41–20. No one thought UCLA had a prayer against such a powerhouse.

But Bruin quarterback John Sciarra wouldn't give up. After a discouraging first half in which his team gained only 48 yards, Sciarra began throwing the ball. In the third quarter he threw two touchdown passes—one for 67 yards. His running back, Wendell

UCLA's Wendell Tyler (22) flips over some Ohio State defenders for a five-yard gain.

Charley Taylor snares a pass for the Redskins in the 1972 NFL championship game against Dallas.

Tyler, ran 57 yards for a third touchdown in the fourth quarter. By the end of the game UCLA had pulled the biggest upset of the football year, beating Ohio State, 23–10.

The Bruins have often taken second place to Southern Cal in football. But their best teams have been superb. Under coach Red Sanders they won the national championship in 1954. And in 1965, with quarterback Gary Beban, they upset an undefeated Michigan State team in the Rose Bowl.

UCLA, a campus of the University of California, is located in the Westwood section of Los Angeles. Called the Bruins to distinguish them from the Golden Bears of the University of California at Berkeley, the UCLA teams play their home games at the Los Angeles Coliseum, which they share with the University of Southern California and the Los Angeles Rams. The school colors are navy blue and gold.

Washington Redskins

The roar of the big crowd filled the Washington stadium as the Redskins huddled around quarterback Billy Kilmer. On this December day in 1972 the Washington team and the Dallas Cowboys were playing for the championship of the National Football Con-

153

ference. The winner would go to the Super Bowl.

Washington had built a slim 3–0 lead. Billy Kilmer had just dropped a pass into the hands of his favorite wide receiver, Charley Taylor, and the ball sat only 15 yards from the goal line. Now, in the huddle, Kilmer called for another pass play.

Charley Taylor was ready on the line of scrimmage. On the snap he veered toward the goal posts. He swung his head and saw the brown bullet whizzing toward him. Charley's long fingers snared the spinning ball and he tumbled into the end zone. Thousands of Redskin fans stood and yelled happily. Their beloved "Over the Hill Gang" was leading, 9–0.

The Gang beat the Cowboys, 26–3, and went on to the Super Bowl. There the Miami Dolphins managed to bat away Kilmer's passes, and flatten Larry Brown, the Gang's best rusher. The Dolphins won, 14–7. But in Washington the Redskin fans talked proudly of the team that had mistakenly been dubbed the "Over the Hill Gang." The Gang had brought back some fond memories of great Redskin teams.

The Redskins trace their ancestry to a Boston team that joined the NFL in 1928, dropped out after a season, then came back in 1932. One of the team's owners was George Preston Marshall. A born showman, he loved to put on dazzling half-time shows with bands blaring, majorettes strutting, and cheerleaders leaping. But despite all the hoopla, his Boston team drew few fans—even when it won the NFL's Eastern championship in 1936. (It lost to Green Bay, 21–6, in the game for the NFL title.)

In 1937, Marshall moved the Redskins to Washington. His marching band wore Indian bonnets and his cheerleaders pranced around in mock Indian war dances. He signed an All-America passer from Texas, Sammy Baugh, and made him wear a cowboy hat when he came to Washington. Marshall loudly proclaimed that this "Slingin' Sam" would be the world's greatest passer.

For once a showman's hyperbole proved accurate. Slingin' Sam slung passes that darted as straight as a string into the hands of receivers such as lanky end Wayne Milner. In Baugh's first season, 1937, the Redskins faced the Chicago Bears for the NFL championship. Late in the game the Redskins were losing, 21–7. Then Slingin' Sam flung three touchdown passes in seven minutes and the Redskins won, 28–21, capturing the NFL title.

In 1940 the Redskins again met the Bears for the NFL title. The Bears, roaring out of the newfangled T formation, buried Washington, 73–0. Early in that game Baugh tossed a pass that Milner dropped in the end zone. Later Sammy was asked if the game might have turned out differently if the pass had been caught. "Yup," drawled Sammy, "the score would have been 73–7."

In 1942, Sammy and his Redskins avenged that humiliation by beating the Bears, 14–6, for the championship. The following year the Bears bounced back to beat Washington, 41–21, for the title. In 1945 Washington won its fifth Eastern title in nine years but lost to Cleveland, the Western winner, in the title game, 15–14.

Baugh retired and the Redskins tasted the dust of the new NFL leaders. During the 1950s and 1960s the Redskins were nearly always at the end of the line. Then in 1971 they got a new coach, George Allen. He saw that the Redskins had only three great players—quarterback Sonny Jurgensen, rusher Larry Brown, and pass catcher Charley Taylor. So he purchased a pack of older players from other teams. The players were so old that people said they were "washed up" or "over the hill." The fans laughed and started calling the team the "Over the Hill Gang." They stopped laughing when the Gang racked up a 9–4–1 record in 1971, Washington's best since 1942.

The Redskins were now playing in the

Sonny Jurgensen, one of the players who helped bring new glory to the Redskins in the 1970s.

NFC's Eastern Division. Billy Kilmer had succeeded Jurgensen and led the Gang to that January 1973 Super Bowl where they lost to Miami. During the next few years the Gang was among the NFL's most respected teams. In 1974 and 1976 the Redskins battled into the playoffs. But each time they fell short of the Super Bowl.

The Redskins play in Robert F. Kennedy Stadium, which seats 55,004 and is located in Washington D.C. The team colors are burgundy and gold.

weak side

The side of a formation on which there are fewer linemen (*see* unbalanced line) or fewer receivers.

wild-card team

A team that qualifies for the NFL playoffs by finishing with the best season record of the three second-place teams in its conference. The wild card team then joins its conference's three division winners in the playoffs.

World Football League

The WFL began in 1974 with 12 teams. They included the Chicago Fire, the Detroit Wheels, the Memphis Ironmen, and the New York Stars. By offering a good deal of money to NFL players, the WFL lured to its teams such NFL stars as Paul Warfield, Jim Kiick, and Larry Csonka. At first the WFL seemed a startling success. Owners reported that as many as 50,000 people were attending the games. Then newspapermen discovered that most of those people had been let into the games with free tickets.

With only a few dollars coming into the box office, teams couldn't pay their players. One team filed into its dressing room after a game and saw their extra uniforms being carted away. A laundry was taking the uniforms as payment for the cleaning bill.

The WFL's first season ended with the Birmingham Americans defeating the Florida Blazers for the 1974 WFL championship. By one estimate the owners had lost $20 million. The league was reorganized and began a 1975 season. But before half the games had been played, the World Football League went out of existence.

zone defense

A pass defense in which each defensive back is responsible for covering an area (or zone) of the field. Another type of pass defense is the man-to-man, in which each defensive back covers a particular pass receiver.

About the Authors

Larry Lorimer has been an editor of sports books for both young readers and adults for many years. He also compiled and contributed notes to *Breaking In,* a very popular sports anthology published by Random House in 1974. He is presently pursuing a career as free-lance author and editor in New York City, where he lives with his wife and two children.

John Devaney has written more than twenty sports books, including *Star Pass Receivers of the NFL, Super Bowl!,* and *The Story of Basketball.* He also collaborated with Bob Cousy on a recent book entitled *The Killer Instinct.* Like Mr. Lorimer, he too lives in New York City with his family.

PHOTOGRAPH CREDITS: John E. Biever, 57, 101; Vernon J. Biever, 1, 2, 48 (right), 73, 78, 91, 94; Clifton Boutelle, 33, 59, 135, 139, 145, 146; Rich Clarkson for *Sports Illustrated,* 108; Dick Darcey/Camera 5, 132; Malcolm W. Emmons, 4, 15, 18, 30, 36, 38, 63, 83 (both), 84, 86, 93, 100, 107, 138, 141; Notre Dame, 126; Pictorial Parade, 64; Ken Regan/Camera 5, 10-11, 88, 117, 155; Fred Roe, 17, 99; United Press International, 8-9, 24, 28, 32, 42-43, 48 (left), 54, 61, 74-75, 85, 87, 90, 96, 97, 102, 106, 114, 130, 136, 147, 149, 151, 152, 153; University of Illinois Sports Information Department, 55; Wide World, 12, 14, 16, 22, 37, 45, 68, 75, 79, 82, 103, 116, 129.

Cover photo by Walter Iooss, Jr., for *Sports Illustrated,* © Time Inc.

INDEX